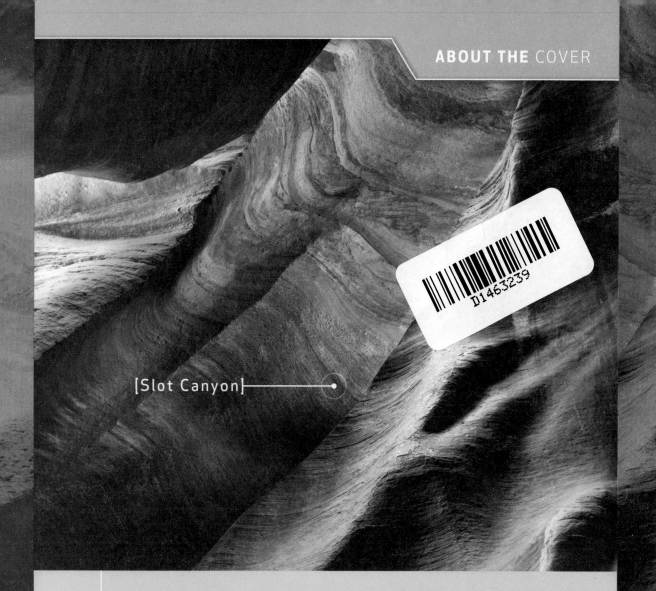

[Slot Canyon]

ZION NATIONAL PARK, UTAH

Zion National Park is located in Utah. The national park is well known for its rock formations, but is most famous for its slot canyons. A slot canyon, such as the one in the picture, is a narrow canyon formed by weathering and erosion. Over millions of years, moving water eroded the rock to form the narrow canyon.

A slot canyon is much deeper than it is wide. Most slot canyons form in sandstone, limestone, or other easily-eroded rocks.

Beware! Slot canyons should be avoided if there is any sign of rain. Flash floods can quickly fill up the canyons with water, making them very dangerous.

NATIONAL GEOGRAPHIC
SCIENCE

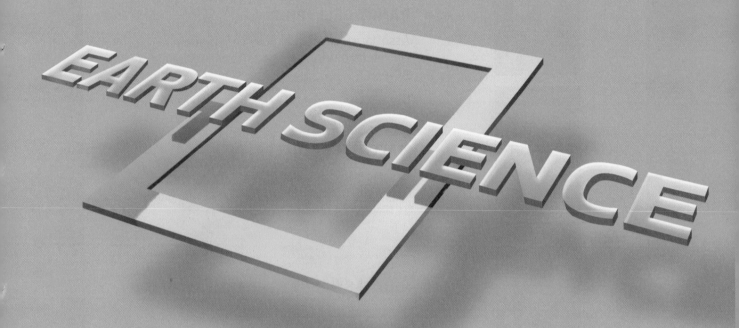

EARTH SCIENCE

PROGRAM AUTHORS

Kathy Cabe Trundle, Ph.D.

Randy Bell, Ph.D.

Malcolm B. Butler, Ph.D.

Judith S. Lederman, Ph.D.

David W. Moore, Ph.D.

NATIONAL GEOGRAPHIC LEARNING

CENGAGE Learning

Program Authors

KATHY CABE TRUNDLE, PH.D.

Associate Professor of Early Childhood Science
Education, The School of Teaching and Learning,
The Ohio State University, Columbus, Ohio
SCIENCE

RANDY BELL, PH.D.

Associate Professor of Science Education,
University of Virginia, Charlottesville, Virginia
SCIENCE

MALCOLM B. BUTLER, PH.D.

Associate Professor of Science Education,
University of South Florida, St. Petersburg, Florida
SCIENCE

JUDITH SWEENEY LEDERMAN, PH.D.

Director of Teacher Education,
Associate Professor of Science Education,
Department of Mathematics and Science Education,
Illinois Institute of Technology, Chicago, Illinois
SCIENCE

DAVID W. MOORE, PH.D.

Professor of Education,
College of Teacher Education and Leadership,
Arizona State University, Tempe, Arizona
LITERACY

Program Reviewers

Amani Abuhabsah
Teacher
Dawes Elementary
Chicago, IL

Maria Aida Alani, Ph.D.
Elementary Science
Instructional Coordinator
Austin Independent
School District
Austin, TX

Jamillah Bakr
Science Mentor Teacher
Cambridge Public Schools
Cambridge, MA

Gwendolyn Battle-Lavert
Assistant Professor of Education
Indiana Wesleyan University
Marion, IN

Carmen Beadles
Retired Science Instructional
Coach
Dallas Independent School
District
Dallas, TX

Andrea Blake-Garrett, Ed.D.
Science Educational Consultant
Newark, NJ

Lori Bowen
Science Specialist
Fayette County Schools
Lexington, KY

Pamela Breitberg
Lead Science Teacher
Zapata Academy
Chicago, IL

Carol Brueggeman
K–5 Science/Math Resource
Teacher
District 11
Colorado Springs, CO

Miranda Carpenter
Teacher, MS Academy Leader
Imagine School
Bradenton, FL

Program Reviewers continued
on page iv.

Acknowledgments

Grateful acknowledgment is given to the authors, artists, photographers, museums, publishers, and agents for permission to reprint copyrighted material. Every effort has been made to secure the appropriate permission. If any omissions have been made or if corrections are required, please contact the Publisher.

Illustrator Credits
All illustrations by Precision Graphics. All maps by Mapping Specialists.

Photographic Credits
Front Cover Whit Richardson/Aurora Photos/Corbis.

Credits continue on page EM17.

National Geographic Learning |
Cengage Learning
NGL.Cengage.com

888-915-3276

Printed in the USA.
RR Donnelley

ISBN: 978-1-3051-2055-6

16 17 18 19 20 21 22 23

10 9 8 7 6 5 4 3

Samuel Carpenter
Teacher
Coonley Elementary
Chicago, IL

Diane E. Comstock
Science Resource Teacher
Cheyenne Mountain School
District
Colorado Springs, CO

Kelly Culbert
K–5 Science Lab Teacher
Princeton Elementary
Orange County, FL

Karri Dawes
K–5 Science Instructional
Support Teacher
Garland Independent
School District
Garland, TX

Richard Day
Science Curriculum Specialist
Union Public Schools
Tulsa, OK

Michele DeMuro
Teacher/Educational
Consultant
Monroe, NY

Richard Ellenburg
Science Lab Teacher
Camelot Elementary
Orlando, FL

Beth Faulkner
Brevard Public Schools
Elementary Training Cadre,
Science Point of Contact,
Teacher, NBCT
Apollo Elementary
Titusville, FL

Kim Feltre
Science Supervisor
Hillsborough School District
Newark, NJ

Judy Fisher
Elementary Curriculum
Coordinator
Virginia Beach Schools
Virginia Beach, VA

Anne Z. Fleming
Teacher
Coonley Elementary
Chicago, IL

Becky Gill, Ed.D.
Principal/Elementary Science
Coordinator
Hough Street Elementary
Barrington, IL

Rebecca Gorinac
Elementary Curriculum Director
Port Huron Area Schools
Port Huron, MI

Anne Grall Reichel Ed. D.
Educational Leadership/
Curriculum and Instruction
Consultant
Barrington, IL

Mary Haskins, Ph.D.
Professor of Biology
Rockhurst University
Kansas City, MO

Arlene Hayman
Teacher
Paradise Public School District
Las Vegas, NV

DeLene Hoffner
Science Specialist, Science
Methods Professor,
Regis University
Academy 20 School District
Colorado Springs, CO

Cindy Holman
District Science Resource
Teacher
Jefferson County Public
Schools
Louisville, KY

Sarah E. Jesse
Instructional Specialist for
Hands-on Science
Rutherford County Schools
Murfreesboro, TN

Dianne Johnson
Science Curriculum Specialist
Buffalo City School District
Buffalo, NY

Kathleen Jordan
Teacher
Wolf Lake Elementary
Orlando, FL

Renee Kumiega
Teacher
Frontier Central School District
Hamburg, NY

Edel Maeder
K–12 Science Curriculum
Coordinator
Greece Central School District
North Greece, NY

Trish Meegan
Lead Teacher
Coonley Elementary
Chicago, IL

Donna Melpolder
Science Resource Teacher
Chatham County Schools
Chatham, NC

Melissa Mishovsky
Science Lab Teacher
Palmetto Elementary
Orlando, FL

Nancy Moore
Educational Consultant
Port Stanley, Ontario, Canada

Melissa Ray
Teacher
Tyler Run Elementary
Powell, OH

Shelley Reinacher
Science Coach
Auburndale Central Elementary
Auburndale, FL

Kevin J. Richard
Science Education Consultant,
Office of School Improvement
Michigan Department
of Education
Lansing, MI

Cathe Ritz
Teacher
Louis Agassiz Elementary
Cleveland, OH

Rose Sedely
Science Teacher
Eustis Heights Elementary
Eustis, FL

Robert Sotak, Ed.D.
Science Program Director,
Curriculum and Instruction
Everett Public Schools
Everett, WA

Karen Steele
Teacher
Salt Lake City School District
Salt Lake City, UT

Deborah S. Teuscher
Science Coach and
Planetarium Director
Metropolitan School District
of Pike Township
Indianapolis, IN

Michelle Thrift
Science Instructor
Durrance Elementary
Orlando, FL

Cathy Trent
Teacher
Ft. Myers Beach Elementary
Ft. Myers Beach, FL

Jennifer Turner
Teacher
PS 146
New York, NY

Flavia Valente
Teacher
Oak Hammock Elementary
Port St. Lucie, FL

Deborah Vannatter
District Coach, Science
Specialist
Evansville Vanderburgh School
Corporation
Evansville, IN

Katherine White
Science Coordinator
Milton Hershey School
Hershey, PA

Sandy Yellenberg
Science Coordinator
Santa Clara County Office of
Education
Santa Clara, CA

Hillary Zeune de Soto
Science Strategist
Lunt Elementary
Las Vegas, NV

CONTENTS

CHAPTER
3

TECHTREK
myNGconnect.com

Student eEdition **Vocabulary Games** **Digital Library** **Enrichment Activities**

EARTH
SCIENCE

Earth science investigates all aspects of our home planet from its changing surface, to its rocks, minerals, water, and other resources. It also includes the study of Earth's atmosphere, weather, and climates. As Earth is an object in space, Earth science also includes the study of Earth's relationship with the sun, moon, and stars. People who study our planet are called Earth scientists.

You will learn about these aspects of Earth science in this unit:

HOW DO EARTH AND ITS MOON CREATE CYCLES?

Earth scientists study how Earth and its moon rotate and revolve. The movements of Earth cause day and night, and the seasons. The moon's revolution around Earth results in phases of the moon. Eclipses and tides are also events caused by the cyclical movements of Earth and its moon.

WHAT MAKES UP THE SOLAR SYSTEM?

Our part of the universe, the solar system, includes many different kinds of objects. Revolving around the nearest star—the sun—you will find planets, moons, asteroids, dwarf planets, and comets. Earth scientists study these objects and Earth's relationship with them.

HOW ARE ROCKS AND MINERALS IDENTIFIED?

Earth scientists classify rocks and minerals so they can tell them apart. Minerals are identified based on their properties, such as hardness, luster, streak, cleavage, and color. Rocks are identified and classified based on how they form.

HOW CAN WE PROTECT EARTH'S RESOURCES?

Earth has all the resources people need to live. Renewable resources, and nonrenewable resources. Earth scientists study how people can protect Earth's resources by using renewable resources wisely, and by reducing, reusing, and recycling nonrenewable resources.

HOW ARE WEATHER AND THE WATER CYCLE CONNECTED?

Weather is the condition of the atmosphere around you. Water in the atmosphere is a part of weather. Earth's water is used over and over again as it cycles through a system called the water cycle. Through evaporation, condensation, and precipitation, water is constantly reused. Earth scientists study weather and the role of water in it.

MEET A SCIENTIST

Tim Samaras: Severe-Storm Researcher

Tim Samaras is a severe-storm researcher and a National Geographic Emerging Explorer. Tim studies tornadoes in order to give people better warning of future storms. He also studies tornadoes to find out more about when, where, and how they form.

Tim invented weather-measurement probes that record data such as humidity, air pressure, temperature, wind speed, and direction. Sometimes the probes have cameras inside that can record the inside of a tornado! Tim's goal is to place a weather probe in the path of a tornado. This can sometimes be dangerous work as he has to get close to a tornado. Tim uses probes and other weather devices to help predict when and where a tornado is going to hit.

About his work with tornadoes, Tim says, "Data from the probes help us understand tornado dynamics and how they form. With this information, we can make more precise forecasts and ultimately give people earlier warnings."

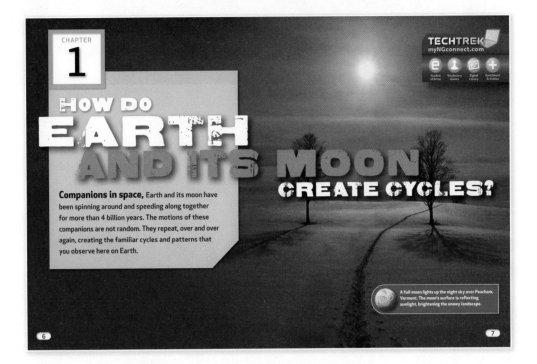

CHAPTER

1

HOW DO
EARTH
AND ITS MOON
CREATE CYCLES?

Companions in space, Earth and its moon have been spinning around and speeding along together for more than 4 billion years. The motions of these companions are not random. They repeat, over and over again, creating the familiar cycles and patterns that you observe here on Earth.

TECHTREK
myNGconnect.com

A full moon lights up the night sky over Peacham, Vermont. The moon's surface is reflecting sunlight, brightening the snowy landscape.

After reading Chapter 1, you will be able to:

- Explain that Earth and the other planets rotate on their axis. **PLANETS ROTATE**

- Explain the apparent motion of the planets and stars. **PLANETS ROTATE**

- Describe how Earth and the other planets revolve around the sun.
  PLANETS ORBIT THE SUN

- Describe the motion of planets is due to gravity. **PLANETS ORBIT THE SUN**

- Explain how Earth's orbit and tilt cause the seasons. **PLANETS ORBIT THE SUN**

- Explain that the moon orbits Earth in about a month. **MOONS ORBIT PLANETS**

- Explain the phases of the moon. **MOONS ORBIT PLANETS**

- Explain lunar and solar eclipses, and tides. **ECLIPSES AND TIDES**

- Science in a Snap! Explain lunar and solar eclipses, and tides. **ECLIPSES AND TIDES**

HOW DO EARTH AND ITS

Companions in space, Earth and its moon have been spinning around and speeding along together for more than 4 billion years. The motions of these companions are not random. They repeat, over and over again, creating the familiar cycles and patterns that you observe here on Earth.

TECHTREK
myNGconnect.com

Student
eEdition

Vocabulary
Games

Digital
Library

Enrichment
Activities

MOON
CREATE CYCLES?

A full moon lights up the night sky over Peacham, Vermont. The moon's surface is reflecting sunlight, brightening the snowy landscape.

SCIENCE VOCABULARY

rotation (rō-TĀ-shun)

Rotation is the act of spinning around. (p. 10)

One complete rotation of Earth takes 24 hours.

apparent motion (uh-PAIR-ant MŌ-shun)

An object's **apparent motion** is the way it appears to move, not whether or how it actually moves. (p. 12)

To the boy on the ride, the people watching appear blurry because they have apparent motion.

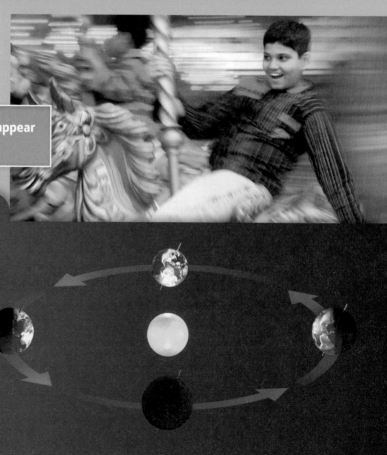

revolution (rev-u-LŪ-shun)

Revolution is the act of moving around another object. (p. 16)

One complete revolution of Earth around the sun takes one year.

my Science Vocabulary

apparent motion
(uh-PAIR-ant MŌ-shun)

eclipse
(i-KLIPS)

hemisphere
(HEM-us-fear)

orbit
(OR-bit)

revolution
(rev-u-LŪ-shun)

rotation
(rō-TĀ-shun)

TECHTREK
myNGconnect.com

Vocabulary
Games

orbit (OR-bit)

An **orbit** is the path one object takes around another object. (p. 16)

Each planet follows an orbit around the sun.

hemisphere (HEM-us-fear)

A **hemisphere** is one-half of Earth's surface, usually above or below the Equator. (p. 18)

When it is summer in the Northern Hemisphere, it is winter in the Southern Hemisphere.

eclipse (i-KLIPS)

An **eclipse** is the blocking of light shining from one object in space onto another. (p. 30)

When the moon blocks the sun's light from shining on Earth, a solar eclipse occurs.

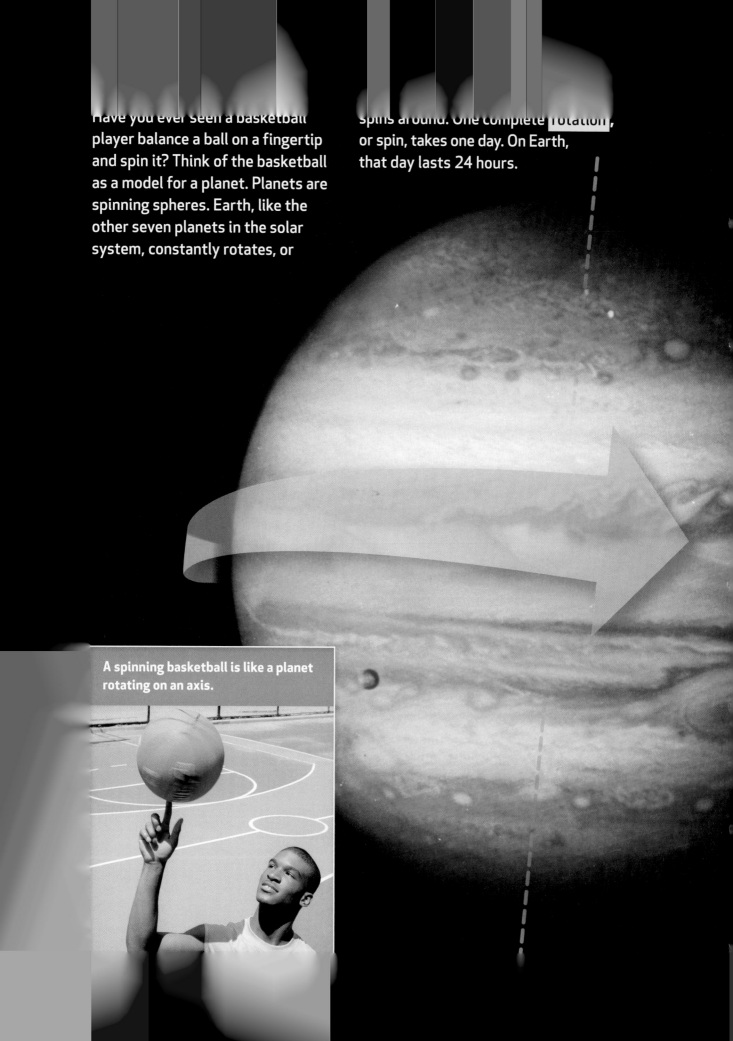

Have you ever seen a basketball player balance a ball on a fingertip and spin it? Think of the basketball as a model for a planet. Planets are spinning spheres. Earth, like the other seven planets in the solar system, constantly rotates, or spins around. One complete rotation, or spin, takes one day. On Earth, that day lasts 24 hours.

A spinning basketball is like a planet rotating on an axis.

Planets rotate at different speeds, so the time it takes each planet to complete one rotation varies. That means the length of a day on each planet varies.

Earth rotates from west to east around an axis, an imaginary line that runs through its North Pole and South Pole. The axis is tilted at an angle.

Each of the other planets also rotates on an axis. Most rotate from west to east, just like Earth. The tilts of the planets vary, though. Mercury's axis does not tilt at all. Uranus, on the other hand, is so tilted that it appears to rotate on its side! You can observe Jupiter's axis in the photo. Compare its axis to Earth's. Which planet is more tilted?

Earth rotates at least as fast as a jet airplane. However, Earth's speed varies. The area near the Equator rotates faster than the area near the poles.

Jupiter is many times larger than Earth, but it rotates much faster. A day on Jupiter lasts about 10 hours.

If you make a "thumbs up" sign with your right hand and then tilt it, your thumb represents Earth's axis. Your fingers show the direction of rotation of the planet.

The Apparent Motion of Objects

Have you ever ridden on a merry-go-round? The people and objects on the ground seem to go by you, instead of the other way around. What you see is their apparent motion. Apparent motion is the way something appears to move.

Earth's rotation is like that of a merry-go-round. Because Earth is so much bigger, you don't sense its rotation. You feel as if you are staying still and everything else is moving. As you look out into space, Earth's rotation gradually changes your viewpoint. You see one part of the sky and then rotate away from it to see another. Your motion makes it seem as if the objects you see—the sun, the stars, the moon—are moving past you. The objects have apparent motion.

Whether or not something looks like it is moving depends on where you are. Which objects in this photo have apparent motion?

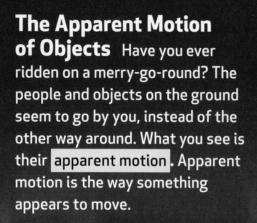

The Sun's Apparent Motion

Throughout the day, you can observe the sun's apparent motion. The sun appears to move east to west because you are moving west to east. In the morning, it seems to rise toward the east. It is low in the sky. With sunlight coming from this direction, shadows of objects are long and stretch toward the west. At midday the sun is high in the sky. Shadows are short. By the late afternoon, the sun is low in the western sky. At this angle, the sun creates long shadows that stretch toward the east. Then, as you rotate into darkness, the sun appears to set toward the west. It is nighttime—time to watch the apparent motion of the stars.

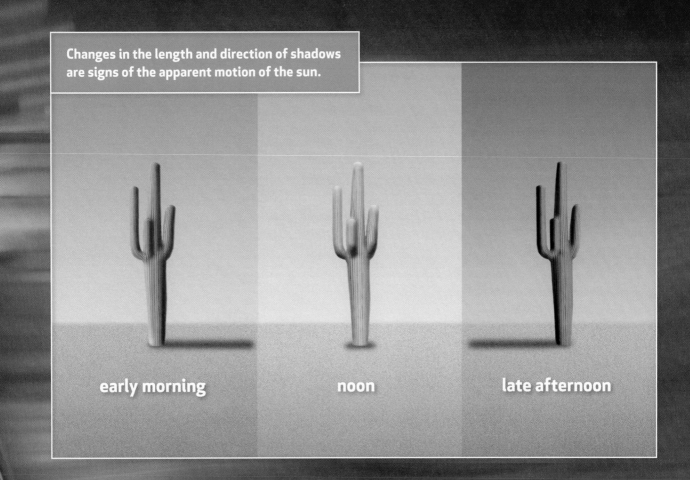

Changes in the length and direction of shadows are signs of the apparent motion of the sun.

early morning   noon   late afternoon

Stars and Planets Like the sun, nearly every star seen from Earth appears to move in the sky. Most stars and constellations, or star patterns, appear to travel across the sky in a curve. They rise toward the east and set toward the west.

Stars in different areas of the sky appear to move differently. All of them do seem to travel in a curve. But some stars near the North Pole move around in a tight circle, never rising or setting. Polaris is a star directly over the North Pole.

Mars ⟶

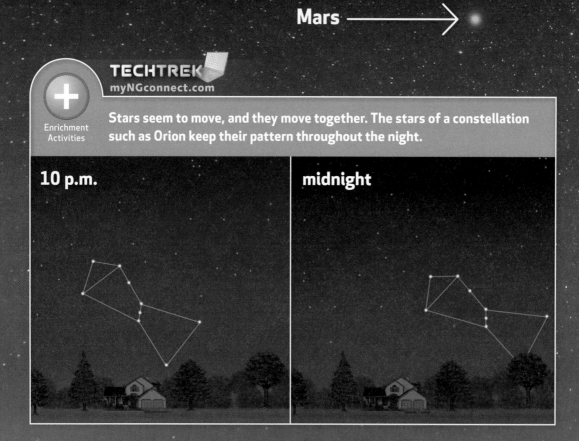

Enrichment
Activities

Stars seem to move, and they move together. The stars of a constellation such as Orion keep their pattern throughout the night.

10 p.m.

midnight

night, the whole starry sky would appear to rotate counterclockwise around Polaris. The stars appear to move this way because Earth is rotating on its axis, which runs through the North Pole.

Some bright objects in the sky are not stars. They are planets. You can tell planets from stars in two ways. First, planets don't appear to twinkle as stars do because they are closer to Earth. The light reflected from them is perceived by your eye differently than light from the distant stars. Second, planets move independently against the background of the stars. From one night to the next, the planets will appear to change their position among the stars. But stars don't do this. They always seem to move together. For centuries people have observed this motion of the planets. The name *planet* comes from an ancient Greek word for "wanderer."

Orion Constellation

Before You Move On

1. What does *rotation* mean?
2. What causes the apparent motion of the sun and stars?
3. **Apply** Suppose you think an object in the night sky is a planet. What clues might lead you think this?

15

... ., ...
...ving, or moving around the sun. ... makes one complete revolution ...d the sun in one year. The path ... Earth takes as it revolves is ... its orbit . The orbit of each ...t is nearly circular. Observe the ...s of the planets in the diagram. ...ts are different distances from ...un. The time a planet takes to ...ve around the sun depends on ...ar it has to travel.

Why do the planets revolve around the sun? The answer is gravity. Gravity is the attraction, or pull, between any two objects. The strength of gravity depends on the mass of the objects and the distance between them. Think about dropping a pencil. Earth's gravity pulls the pencil down. The pencil also pulls on

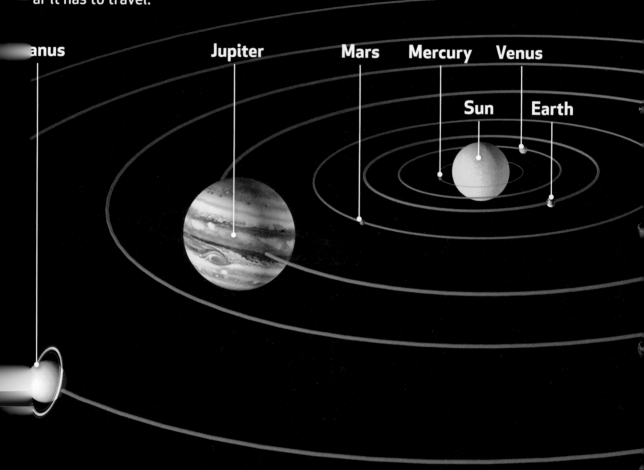

...anus   Jupiter   Mars   Mercury   Venus

Sun   Earth

...length of a year differs from planet to ...et. A year on Earth is about 365 days. At only ...Earth days, Mercury's year is the shortest. ...ich planet do you think has the longest year?

Earth. But Earth has more mass than the pencil. So the pencil falls toward Earth instead of Earth rising up toward the pencil.

The sun's mass is huge. Its gravitational pull on the planets is strong. So why don't Earth and the other planets crash into the sun?

Because the planets are traveling in a straight line through space! This may be hard to imagine. But each planet is pulled toward the sun while it continues to move away in a straight line. The combination of the planet's forward motion and the sun's gravity results in a nearly circular orbit around the sun.

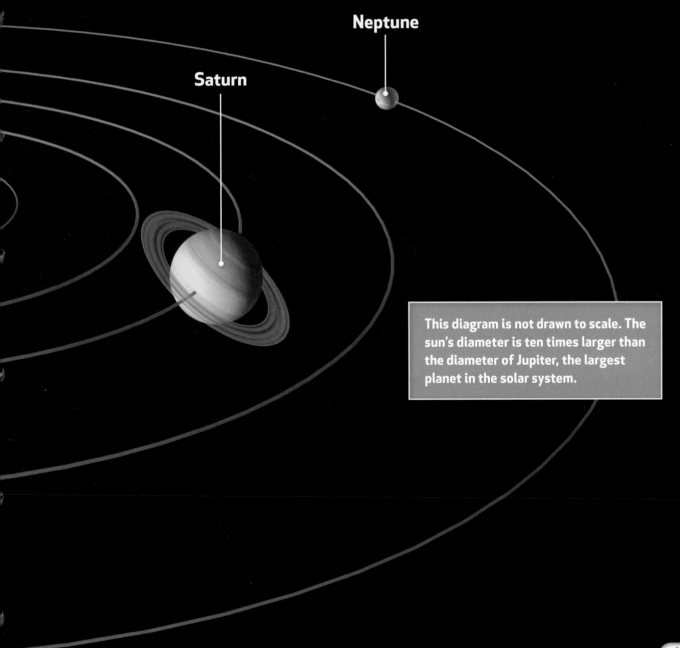

Neptune

Saturn

This diagram is not drawn to scale. The sun's diameter is ten times larger than the diameter of Jupiter, the largest planet in the solar system.

Earth's Tilt and the Seasons

One effect of Earth's orbit around the sun is the seasons. However, the seasonal changes on Earth are caused by Earth's tilt on its axis and not because Earth is farther from the sun at different times of the year. Earth is always tilted in the same direction as it moves around the sun. On one side of Earth's orbit, the North Pole is pointed more toward the sun. On the other side of Earth's orbit, the South Pole is pointed more toward the sun. Usually one hemisphere, or half of Earth, gets more or less direct sunlight than the other.

In the Northern Hemisphere, summer occurs during the time when the North Pole is tilted most toward the sun. Winter occurs during the time when it is tilted most away from the sun. Meanwhile, the Southern Hemisphere always has the opposite season.

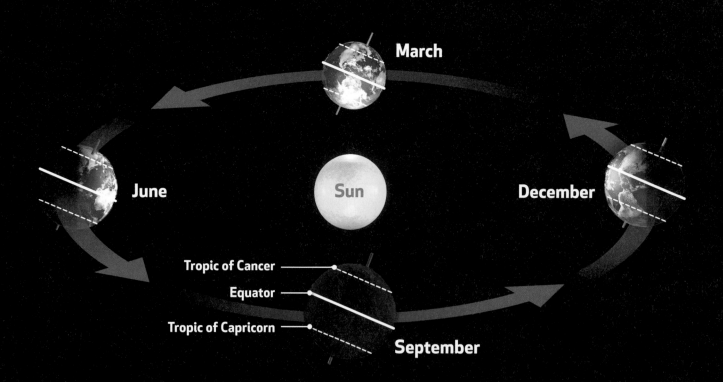

March

June

Sun

December

Tropic of Cancer

Equator

Tropic of Capricorn

September

Latitude affects the seasons too. Latitude is how far north or south of the Equator a place is. In lower latitudes, temperatures do not vary as much as they do at higher latitudes.

In its orbit around the sun, Earth eventually reaches a place where one pole points most directly toward the sun. The maximum amount of sunlight strikes that hemisphere, while the minimum amount strikes the other.

This is called a solstice. The solstices occur twice a year, around June 21 and December 21.

Since Earth's axis always tilts in the same direction, there will be two times when neither pole is pointed toward the sun. This is called an equinox. At an equinox, sunlight shines equally on both hemispheres. The equinoxes occur twice a year, around March 21 and September 21.

DIFFERING AMOUNTS OF **DAYLIGHT HOURS**

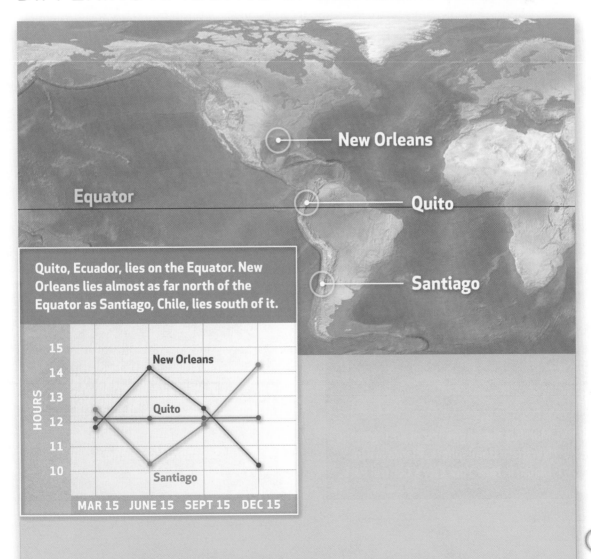

New Orleans

Equator

Quito

Santiago

Quito, Ecuador, lies on the Equator. New Orleans lies almost as far north of the Equator as Santiago, Chile, lies south of it.

New Orleans

Quito

Santiago

HOURS
15
14
13
12
11
10

MAR 15   JUNE 15   SEPT 15   DEC 15

What season is it where you live? Read on to observe why the seasons change during Earth's orbit around the sun.

March Equinox Earth's constant tilt and motion around the sun creates the seasons. Think about March in New York City. Since December, days in the Northern Hemisphere have been getting a little longer. Earth's journey in its orbit has brought the north end of its axis more and more toward the sun. Around the March equinox, the number of daylight hours catches up with the number of nighttime hours.

Each day, the sun is a little higher in the sky. Sunlight is more direct, and shadows at noon are shorter. Temperatures rise as more of the sun's energy warms Earth's surface. The pattern of more sunlight and less dark continues until late June.

Meanwhile, the reverse is happening in the Southern Hemisphere. The days keep getting shorter. By March, they are getting cooler too.

March is the beginning of spring in the Northern Hemisphere. Plants are in bloom in New York City's Central Park.

Sydney, Australia, is in the Southern Hemisphere. Fall begins in March.

June Solstice By the time of the June solstice, the North Pole is pointed more toward the sun than at any other time of year. The Northern Hemisphere gets the most direct sunlight of the year. The sun is highest in the sky. Following the June solstice, days begin to grow shorter again. But the temperature will continue to get warmer for several more weeks. Summer temperatures are the warmest of the year.

In the Southern Hemisphere, days are shortest in June. The South Pole is pointing away from the sun. The sunlight striking Earth's surface is the least direct that it can be. After the solstice, days begin to lengthen. But it will continue to get colder for many weeks to come.

June means cool winter temperatures and the shortest days of the year in Sydney.

On the longest day of the year, Central Park gets more than 15 hours of sunlight.

September Equinox Since the June solstice, days in the Northern Hemisphere have been getting shorter again. After the September equinox, the North Pole is pointing away from the sun. The number of nighttime hours catches up with the number of daylight hours. The decrease in daylight hours continues. As the sun gets lower in the sky each day, sunlight is less and less direct. These changes bring cooler temperatures. Leaves change color. It is fall in the Northern Hemisphere.

In the Southern Hemisphere, days have been getting longer since the June solstice. From the September equinox, Earth's movement brings the South Pole more toward the sun. The number of daylight hours increases over the number of nighttime hours. The sun gets higher in the sky and light is more direct. Temperatures rise. Plants begin to bloom. It is spring in the Southern Hemisphere.

Temperatures begin to get cooler in Central Park around the September equinox which is the beginning of fall.

In Sydney and elsewhere in the Southern Hemisphere, spring begins in September.

December Solstice In December, the north end of Earth's axis is pointed more away from the sun than at any other time of year. The sun is lowest in the sky and sunlight is least direct. At places far north of the Equator, it has been cold for many weeks already. After the December solstice, days will start getting longer again. But it is winter now, the year's coldest season. It will be many more weeks before temperatures begin to rise.

In the Southern Hemisphere, days are longest in December. The South Pole is pointing most toward the sun. The sunlight striking Earth's surface is the most direct that it can be here. After the solstice, days begin to shorten. But it will continue to get warmer for weeks to come. It is summer south of the Equator.

On the shortest day of the year, Central Park gets a little more than nine hours of daylight.

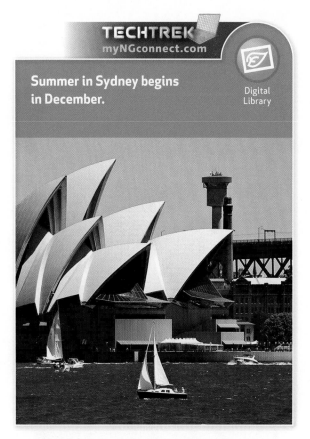

Summer in Sydney begins in December.

Before You Move On

1. Describe Earth's orbit.
2. Explain how Earth's tilt causes the seasons.
3. **Apply** Where might you go to find winter in July? Explain why.

Moons Orbit Planets

Some planets, such as Jupiter and Saturn, have many moons. The planets Mercury and Venus have none. Earth has one. Earth's moon is a satellite—an object that revolves around a planet.

Satellites orbit planets for the same reason that planets orbit the sun—gravity. Gravity is the force that keeps the planets and moons revolving. For example, Earth's larger size makes its gravity stronger than the moon's. Earth holds the moon in its orbit. The moon also follows Earth as Earth revolves around the sun. As with the other planets and their satellites, the sun's powerful gravity keeps both Earth and the moon revolving in a regular and repeating orbit.

Earth's gravity acts on the moon more than the sun's gravity because the moon is much closer to Earth.

Earth's Moon The moon is the closest object to Earth. It is visible during the day and night as it orbits around Earth. Not only does the moon revolve, it also rotates like Earth on an axis. However, the moon rotates much slower than Earth.

The time the moon takes to rotate once and revolve once is the same. This means that one side of the moon always faces Earth. You can see only this side. No human saw the far side of the moon until people could send spacecraft to explore it.

These people in London, England, enjoy a clear view of the moon.

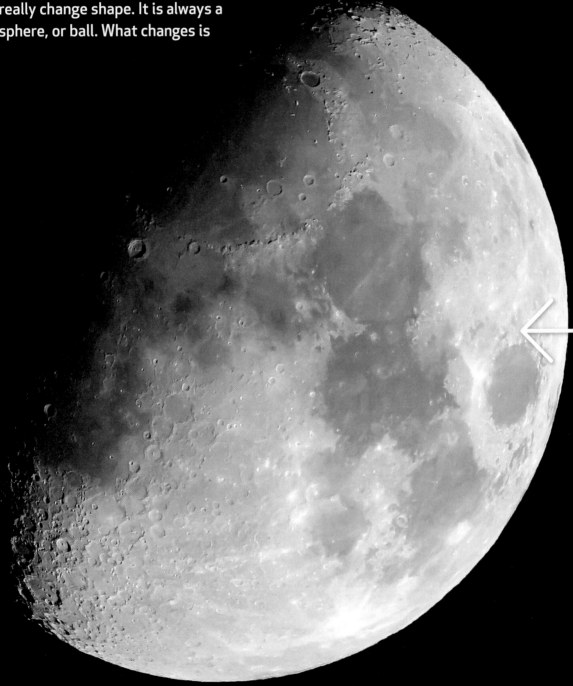

The Moon's Phases If you looked at the moon today or tonight, what shape would it appear to have? Each different shape is a phase of the moon. The phases you see from Earth result from the moon's position in orbit. The moon doesn't really change shape. It is always a sphere, or ball. What changes is how much of its lighted half you can see from Earth. The diagram shows how the positions of the moon, Earth, and the sun affect the shape of the moon you see in the sky.

The moon does not shine its own light. It reflects sunlight. So what is called "moonlight" is really sunlight. The sun shines on the half of the moon that is facing it. From Earth you see changing amounts of this lighted half.

During a new moon, the entire lighted half is facing away from Earth. So none of the moon is visible to people on Earth. During a full moon, the entire lighted half is facing toward Earth. All the other moon phases are the varying amounts of the lighted half that you can see between these two phases. Look at the moon phases pictured below. Imagine what the moon would look like to you at Week 4.

If you were observing the phase of the moon shown in the photograph, you would see most of the lighted side.

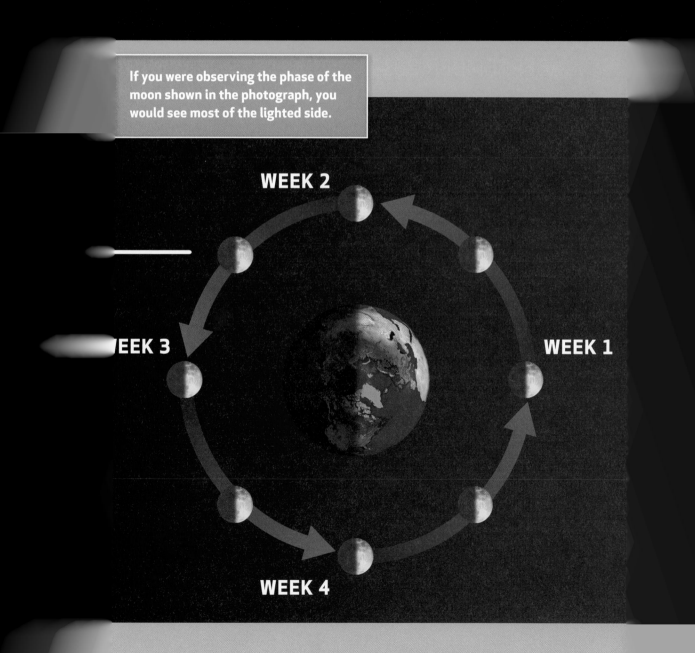

WEEK 2

WEEK 3

WEEK 1

WEEK 4

Predicting Phases Suppose you observed and drew the moon every night for about 30 days. Your moon chart would look something like the picture on this page. The moon completes one cycle of phases about every 30 days.

The pattern of phases, or lighted shapes, repeats. It is a regular cycle. Because the phases are a repeating cycle, you can predict what the moon will look like tomorrow or a year from now. Early people used the moon cycle to mark off time. The word *month* comes from early words for moon.

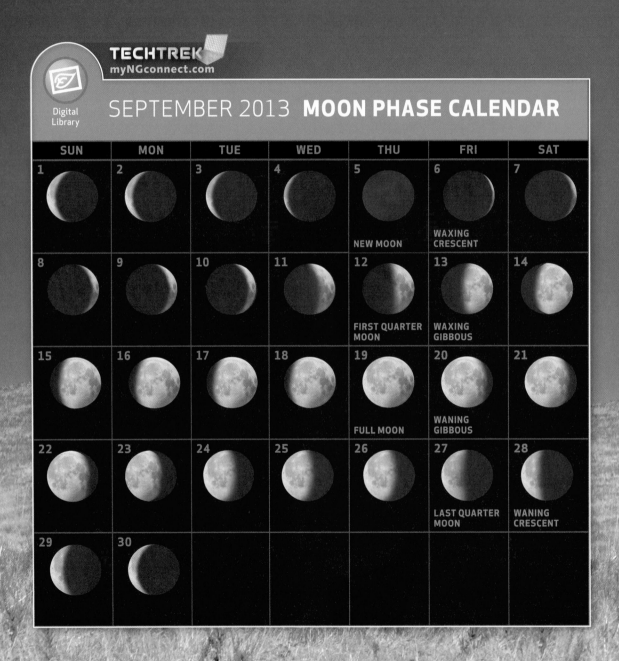

TECHTREK
myNGconnect.com

Digital Library

SEPTEMBER 2013 **MOON PHASE CALENDAR**

SUN	MON	TUE	WED	THU	FRI	SAT
1	2	3	4	5 NEW MOON	6 WAXING CRESCENT	7
8	9	10	11	12 FIRST QUARTER MOON	13 WAXING GIBBOUS	14
15	16	17	18	19 FULL MOON	20 WANING GIBBOUS	21
22	23	24	25	26	27 LAST QUARTER MOON	28 WANING CRESCENT
29	30					

The Moon's Origin Where did the moon come from? Scientists believe it formed from an outer-space crash that happened billions of years ago. When the Earth was young, a small planet about the size of Mars collided with it. The impact destroyed the small planet and forced huge amounts of hot, rocky debris into orbit around Earth. Over time, gravity collected the material into a sphere shape, forming the moon.

ONE HYPOTHESIS OF **HOW THE MOON FORMED**

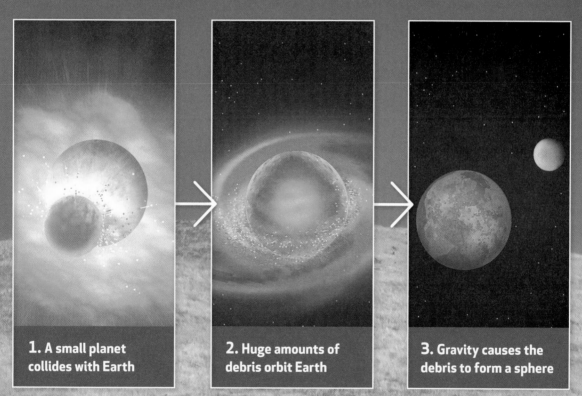

1. A small planet collides with Earth

2. Huge amounts of debris orbit Earth

3. Gravity causes the debris to form a sphere

Before You Move On

1. What is a moon phase?
2. How does the moon's rotation determine the side of it that we see?
3. **Analyze** If there is a first quarter moon tonight, what phase will the moon be in about two weeks from tonight?

Eclipses and Tides

Solar Eclipses The sun is huge when compared with the moon. About 64 million moons would fit inside the sun! Yet sometimes the moon blocks your view of the sun. This event is called an `eclipse` . An eclipse is the blocking of light shining from one object in space onto another. Just as you can block out your view of a friend's face across the room with your thumb, the tinier moon can block out the sun because the moon is much closer to Earth.

About once a month the moon's orbit takes it between the sun and Earth. This is the new moon phase. Usually the moon is a little above or a little below the line of view between Earth and the sun. However, sometimes the moon moves directly in line between Earth and the sun. When the moon is in this position, it blocks sunlight from falling on part of Earth. Look at the diagram to see how they line up during a solar eclipse.

A total eclipse of the sun. The halo of light behind the moon is the sun's corona, or outer atmosphere.

A solar eclipse can be total or partial, depending on how much of the sun the moon blocks out. A total solar eclipse is observed where the moon blocks the entire sun. The sky darkens, and only the sun's bright corona is visible around the edge of the moon. A partial solar eclipse is observed where the moon blocks only a portion of the sun. From two to five total or partial solar eclipses occur somewhere on Earth every year.

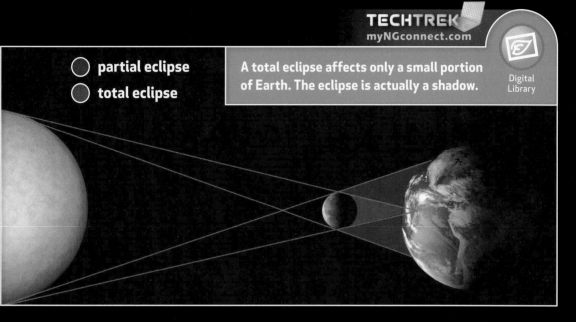

○ partial eclipse
● total eclipse

A total eclipse affects only a small portion of Earth. The eclipse is actually a shadow.

Looking directly at the sun, even during a solar eclipse, can damage your eyes. On July 22, 2009, these people in China wore special glasses to protect their eyes during a solar eclipse.

Lunar Eclipses Like new moons sometimes can cause solar eclipses, Earth can cause lunar eclipses. Recall that a full moon occurs only when Earth is between the moon and the sun. Full moons usually are a little above or a little below Earth's shadow. However, a full moon can sometimes be directly in line with Earth and the sun. If that happens, the moon's orbit crosses Earth's shadow—causing a lunar eclipse. Use the diagram to help you observe what happens during a lunar eclipse.

You know that only the moon's lighted half is visible from Earth. So you might think the moon would disappear from view during a total lunar eclipse. But Earth's shadow affects your view of the moon differently. You can see this in the series of photos.

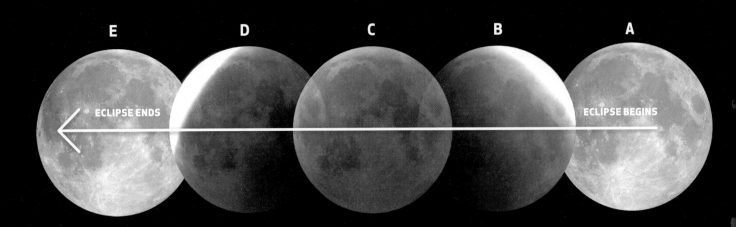

Match the letters in the diagram to each photo of the moon , below, during a total lunar eclipse. Look at how Earth's shadow covers the moon in each photo. The diagram is not to scale. It may look as though a lunar eclipse lasts several days. But it really lasts about 3.5 hours. The total eclipse lasts about 1.25 hours.

As the moon passes into Earth's shadow, its color changes from dusty gray to dark red. The red color comes from Earth's atmosphere. Imagine you were standing on the moon looking back at Earth at the time of total eclipse. You would see a reddish ring all around the planet. Earth's atmosphere bends this red light into Earth's shadow and casts it on the moon.

Like solar eclipses, lunar eclipses can be partial or total. A total lunar eclipse is observed where Earth's shadow falls on the entire moon. A partial lunar eclipse is observed where only a part of the moon is darkened. Lunar eclipses occur less frequently than solar eclipses.

Science in a Snap! Eclipses

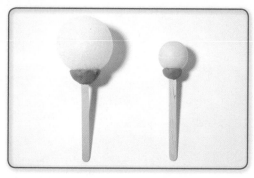

Use clay to fix a large foam Earth to the end of one stick and a table tennis ball moon to the end of another stick.

One person holds a flashlight for the sun. The other person moves the moon between Earth and the sun. When you are finished, switch the position of Earth and the moon and repeat.

What happened to the sunlight striking Earth? What happened to the sunlight striking the moon? How was each like or not like a solar eclipse or a lunar eclipse?

Tides Twice a day along most of the world's oceans, the water level rises in a high tide. Twice a day the water level lowers in a low tide. The tides go back and forth in a cycle: high tide, low tide, high tide, low tide.

Observe the beach in the photo. Look for clues. You can tell it is low tide. Shells, plants, and even a sea star that washed in with high tide water have been left behind.

Tides are the cycle of rising and falling water levels around the world. They are caused by the pull of the moon's gravity. Remember that Earth's stronger gravity keeps the moon in orbit. Yet the moon's gravity also has an effect on Earth—it pulls on Earth's water. This pulling makes Earth's oceans bulge out. The bulges produce tides.

At high tide, this land where the girl is exploring will be covered with water.

Look at the diagram that shows the cycle of tides. During tides, Earth's water bulges out in two areas. It bulges out on the part of Earth facing the moon and on the part facing away from the moon. These bulges cause high tides. You can see the bulges in the diagram.

Meanwhile, two other areas of Earth have low tides. Those are the areas of Earth not in line with the moon. The water in those areas is pulled away by the bulges. Find the areas of low tide in the diagram.

A high tide happens in the area facing the moon because the moon's gravity pulls on Earth's water. But why does high tide happen in the area opposite the moon? The moon's gravity pulls Earth toward the moon. This leaves a bulge of water in the area facing away from the moon.

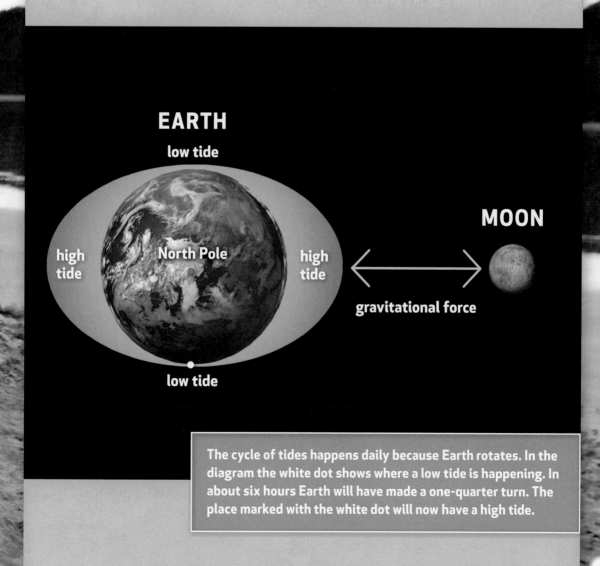

EARTH

low tide

high tide

North Pole

MOON

high tide

gravitational force

low tide

The cycle of tides happens daily because Earth rotates. In the diagram the white dot shows where a low tide is happening. In about six hours Earth will have made a one-quarter turn. The place marked with the white dot will now have a high tide.

The sun's effect on Earth's water is small compared to the moon's because the sun is so far away. But the sun can add to the strength of the moon's pull. In the new moon phase and again in the full moon phase, the moon lines up with the sun. When the sun and the moon are in line with Earth, the sun's gravity combines with the moon's gravity. Their combined pull on Earth's water causes especially high tides. These very high tides are called spring tides. The term "spring tides" has nothing to do with the season. The word spring means "to rise up quickly," like the spring in a bed.

These kayakers paddle near the shore. It is high tide in Canada's Bay of Fundy. The tides here are extreme.

When the moon is in first quarter or third quarter phase, the sun and the moon are pulling at right angles to each other. The sun's gravity lessens the effect of the moon's.

These are called neap tides, when the difference between high and low tide is the smallest. Neap tides occur twice a month.

Compare low tide in this photo with high tide on the facing page. Water levels become even lower and higher during spring tides.

Before You Move On

1. When one side of Earth has a low tide, what kind of tide does the opposite side have?
2. How do the positions of Earth, the moon, and the sun differ between a solar eclipse and a lunar eclipse?
3. **Analyze** If Earth did not rotate but the moon still revolved, what would be the effect on tides?

NATIONAL GEOGRAPHIC

OBSERVING THE SKY
TELESCOPES AND BINOCULARS

Would you like to see the moon up close? Have you wondered what faraway planets and stars really look like? Distances in space are so vast that your eyes alone cannot see things very clearly. Astronomers depend on special instruments, such as telescopes, to observe the moon, planets, and stars in greater detail.

The telescope may be one of the most important inventions in human history. It was officially introduced by Hans Lipperhey in the Netherlands in 1608. Less than a year later, the great Italian astronomer Galileo Galilei started making his own telescopes. Galileo's best telescope was much stronger than anyone else's in Europe. With it, he became the first person to see Jupiter's moons.

The telescope has undergone more than 400 years of improvements. Today's telescopes can magnify objects millions of miles away. You, too, can examine objects in space with binoculars or a telescope. Who knows, you might discover something new! You can explore outer space without ever leaving the ground!

There are two kinds of telescopes. A refracting telescope uses a lens to collect and bend light to focus it. A reflecting telescope, such as this one, uses mirrors.

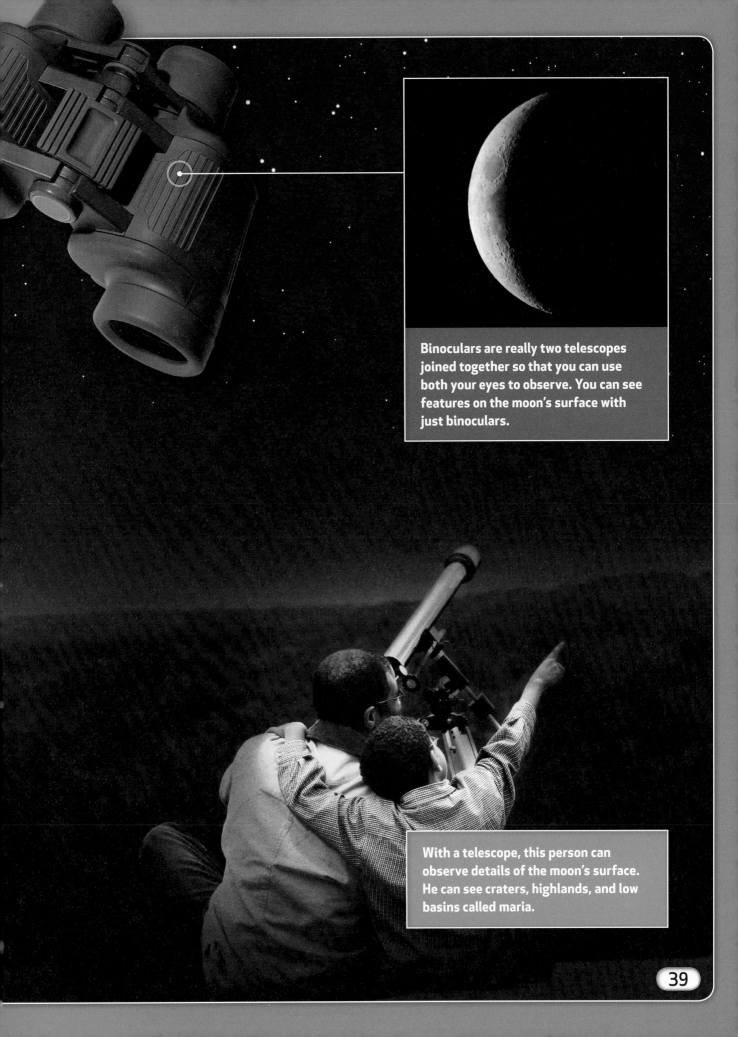

Binoculars are really two telescopes joined together so that you can use both your eyes to observe. You can see features on the moon's surface with just binoculars.

With a telescope, this person can observe details of the moon's surface. He can see craters, highlands, and low basins called maria.

Earth rotates on its axis once a day. Its rotation makes the sun, the moon, and the stars appear to move through the sky. Earth revolves around the sun once a year. Its revolution and tilt on its axis cause the seasons. The moon's revolution around Earth causes us to see the phases of the moon. Eclipses occur when the moon's orbit takes it in line between Earth and the sun or on the opposite side of Earth. The moon's gravity causes tides on Earth.

Big Idea The rotation and revolution of Earth and its moon create daily, monthly, and yearly cycles, including tides, eclipses, and seasons.

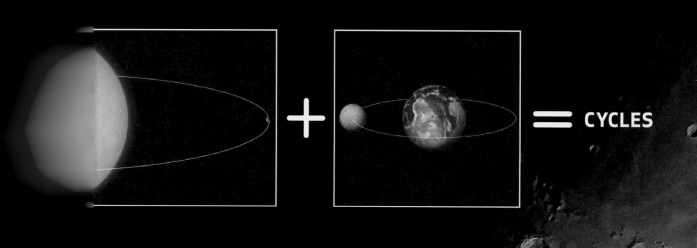

= CYCLES

Vocabulary Review

Match the following terms with the correct definition.

A. **rotation**

B. **revolution**

C. **orbit**

D. **hemisphere**

E. **eclipse**

F. **apparent motion**

1. The path one object takes around another object

2. The blocking of light shining from one object in space onto another

3. The act of spinning around

4. The act of moving around another object

5. The way an object appears to move, not whether or how it actually moves

6. One-half of Earth's surface, usually above or below the Equator

Big Idea Review

1. **Define** What is apparent motion? Describe an example.

2. **Describe** Why does it appear that the moon and stars move in the sky?

3. **Relate** Connect the number of high tides each day to the time it takes for Earth to rotate. How would the number and length of high tides change if Earth took 40 hours to rotate?

4. **Classify** What cycles are caused by the movement of Earth and its moon? Classify them as daily, monthly, and yearly.

5. **Infer** Which two phases could the moon be in if you see half of the lighted portion of the moon?

6. **Draw Conclusions** Suppose you are at a high latitude in July. It is snowing and extremely cold. Which hemisphere are you probably in? Explain how you can tell.

Write About the Moon's Motion

Interpret Diagrams What event does the diagram describe? Explain the parts of the diagram and what they show.

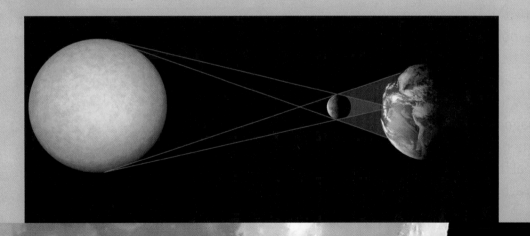

CHAPTER 1 EARTH SCIENCE EXPERT: AEROSPACE ENGINEER

What's the best way to send a mission into outer space? Ask an aerospace engineer.

When you look at the moon, it's hard to imagine a human standing on it. Yet twelve different people have walked on the moon. More than 70 missions have been launched to the moon, and many others have been sent to explore the sun and the planets. All these missions rely on aerospace engineers like Kurt Hack.

Kurt Hack is an aerospace engineer at NASA's Glenn Research Center.

Hack works for the National Aeronautics and Space Administration (NASA). As an aerospace engineer, he looks at the specific goal of a particular mission into space. Is it to track Earth's weather? Or study how the sun interacts with Earth's magnetic field? Or perhaps explore other planets? Then he matches that goal to the best technology available to achieve success.

A space shuttle orbits Earth.

TECHTREK
myNGconnect.com

Student
eEdition

Digital
Library

Aerospace engineering is a cutting-edge field. Discoveries and new inventions are ongoing. Hack especially likes that he works with science, engineering, and the latest technologies around. "Applying the latest technology to the United States' space program just makes it all the more cool," he says.

Hack once participated in the engineering, launch, and operation of a spacecraft called the Advanced Communications Technology Satellite (ACTS). ACTS was launched in space from the Space Shuttle. It orbited Earth for several years.

What does it take to become an aerospace engineer? Hack studied math and science in school and took aerospace engineering courses in college. He has always been interested in space and loved science fiction TV shows when he was young. He also enjoyed learning about explorers in history. Like explorers, aerospace engineers attempt, Hack says, "to do things that have rarely, if ever, been done before."

Aerospace engineers like Kurt Hack are responsible for the design of spacecraft and the instruments that help them work properly.

BECOME AN EXPERT

Extreme Latitudes:
Living in Darkness and Light

Eight countries around the world fall within the Arctic Circle. The people who live at these extreme latitudes have to deal with long periods of sunlight and darkness—as well as freezing winter temperatures!

The Arctic Circle Just what is the Arctic Circle? It's an imaginary line around the North Pole. The Antarctic Circle is a line of the same size around the South Pole. During

Earth's **revolution** around the sun, the areas inside the Arctic and Antarctic Circles have periods of constant sunlight or darkness. Which one—light or dark—depends on the season.

At latitudes above the Arctic Circle, summer days and winter nights may seem endless. And for much of the year, they are endless.

A man builds a campfire, at midnight, on a summer night along the Arctic coast of Alaska.

revolution
Revolution is the act of moving around another object.

TECHTREK
myNGconnect.com

Student
eEdition

Digital
Library

Look at the diagram of Earth as seen from above during summer. Pick any point inside the Arctic Circle. If you watched the sun's **apparent motion** across the sky at the right time of summer from that place, you would see the sun go lower in the sky at night. But the sun wouldn't "set." That's what defines the Arctic Circle. It begins at the first place where the sun doesn't set for 24 hours or longer. The closer to the North Pole you are, the more days of continuous sunlight you will have.

Constant sunlight in summer comes at a big price though—constant winter darkness. Earth's **rotation** doesn't bring places at the highest latitudes out of Earth's shadow for several weeks. Winters near the North Pole are the darkest— and some of the coldest—in the **hemisphere** .

Part of Alaska lies within the Arctic Circle. How do you think Alaskans cope with longer periods of light and dark?

Summer in the Northern hemisphere

Arctic Circle

Sunlight

hemisphere

A **hemisphere** is the half of Earth above or below the Equator.

rotation

Rotation is the act of spinning around.

apparent motion

An object's **apparent motion** is the way it appears to move, not whether or how it actually moves.

45

Alaska in Summer Summer is the season of light in Alaska. In far northern Alaska, at towns like Barrow and Prudhoe Bay, the sun does not set from the middle of May to early August. Many people try to sleep the hours they normally do, but it can be difficult. Some wear eye shades or cover their windows with blackout drapes. Others just continue to work and play for much of the time. It can be fun to practice your golf swing in the middle of the night. Children can play outside until late in the evening. But, it is important to remember to get the right amount of sleep too.

DAYLIGHT HOURS IN BARROW, ALASKA

Barrow is the northernmost town in North America.

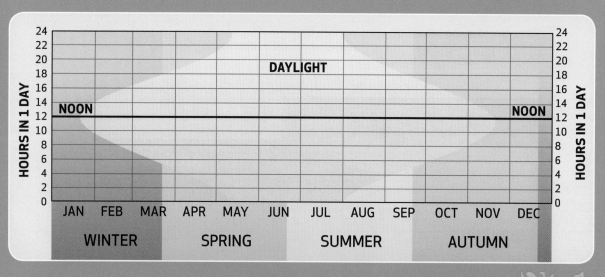

Alaska is known as the Land of the Midnight Sun. Most of it is south of the Arctic Circle. But cities such as Fairbanks and Anchorage are still at very high latitudes. Summer nights are only three or four hours long. Nights are not very dark either. The stars are hard to see. Around June 21, the people of Fairbanks play midnight baseball. The game begins at 10:30 p.m. when the sun is beginning to set, but it remains light enough to play. By the time the game is over, the sun has risen again. Fairbanks also holds a festival, runs a riverboat race, and stages other events to celebrate the sun at night.

Baseball fans watch a midnight sun game.

Every year the longest wheelchair and handcycle race in the world occurs in Alaska during the very long summer days.

Alaska in Winter The darkness begins as Earth orbits into winter in the Northern Hemisphere. People and animals living north of the Arctic Circle won't see the sun for more than 60 days between November and January.

Temperatures can be extremely cold, so many Alaskans spend less time outside. Life slows down. For some Alaskans, winter is the time for dogsledding. Kids still have to go to school though, with or without daylight.

Winter in the Northern Hemisphere

Arctic Circle

Sun

orbit
An **orbit** is the path one object takes around another object.

In places south of the Arctic Circle, the sun shines for only a few hours each day. It rises in the morning and sets after lunch. Cities such as Fairbanks host winter carnivals each year. Where there are electric lights, people can go downhill or cross-country skiing. The constant darkness is good for viewing the northern lights. Tourists from around the world come to Alaska to watch the northern lights. They are almost as popular to see as eclipses.

TECHTREK
myNGconnect.com

Digital
Library

This photo was taken around noon in Barrow, Alaska, during the winter.

eclipse
An **eclipse** is the blocking of light shining from one object in space onto another.

49

Antarctica The land around the South Pole is the continent of Antarctica. Even summer temperatures rarely rise above freezing here. No one lives permanently in Antarctica, but several hundred scientists from different nations stay at research stations for months at a time. Ships and airplanes bring in supplies only during summer. In winter, constant darkness, storms, and sea ice cut off the research stations from the rest of the world.

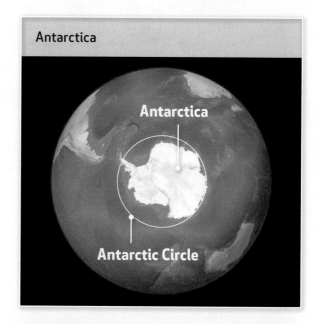

Antarctica

Antarctica

Antarctic Circle

You can barely see the Halley 5 base station at noon on a midwinter's day in Antarctica.

Research outside takes place during the long daylight hours of summer. Scientists camp out on the Antarctic ice. They need to pack and eat more food than they normally would. The extra calories give them the energy to work in this harsh environment. They also wear dark sunglasses to protect their eyes from sunlight reflected off snow and ice. Eventually most scientists get used to the constant daylight.

During dark winter months, scientists spend most of their time staying warm inside the research stations. They have DVDs, CDs, games, and gym facilities to help make life as normal as possible.

TECHTREK
myNGconnect.com

There's plenty of snow in Antarctica for sledding and other activities.

Digital Library

These people are learning how to survive the night in a tent in Antarctica.

SHARE AND COMPARE

Turn and Talk How does the tilt of Earth and its revolution affect life in the extreme north and extreme south? Form a complete answer to this question together with a partner.

Read Select two pages in this section. Practice reading the pages. Then read them aloud to a partner. Talk about why the pages are interesting.

my SCIENCE notebook

Write Write a conclusion that tells the important ideas about what you have learned about living in extreme latitudes. State what you think is the Big Idea of this section. Share what you wrote with a partner. Compare your conclusions. Did your classmate recall that seasons take place at different times depending on where you live?

my SCIENCE notebook

Draw Imagine what it is like living at an extreme latitude during the winter. Draw a picture of an activity you could do outside. Combine your idea with those of your classmates. Create a calendar of events for the month of January.

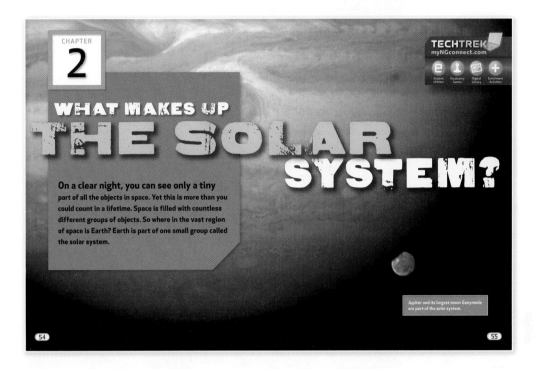

CHAPTER 2

WHAT MAKES UP THE SOLAR SYSTEM?

On a clear night, you can see only a tiny part of all the objects in space. Yet this is more than you could count in a lifetime. Space is filled with countless different groups of objects. So where in the vast region of space is Earth? Earth is part of one small group called the solar system.

TECHTREK
myNGconnect.com
Student eEdition
Vocabulary Games
Digital Library
Enrichment Activities

Jupiter and its largest moon Ganymede are part of the solar system.

54   55

After reading Chapter 2, you will be able to:

- Identify the objects that make up a galaxy. **STARS AND GALAXIES**

- Identify the objects that make up the solar system. **THE SOLAR SYSTEM**

- Identify and compare the planets and moons. **THE INNER PLANETS, THE OUTER PLANETS**

- Recognize that asteroids, dwarf planets, and comets are objects in the solar system.
  OTHER OBJECTS IN THE SOLAR SYSTEM

- Science in a Snap! Identify the objects that make up the solar system. **THE SOLAR SYSTEM**

WHAT MAKES UP THE SO

On a clear night, you can see only a tiny part of all the objects in space. Yet this is more than you could count in a lifetime. Space is filled with countless different groups of objects. So where in the vast region of space is Earth? Earth is part of one small group called the solar system.

LAR SYSTEM?

Jupiter and its largest moon Ganymede are part of the solar system.

SCIENCE VOCABULARY

star (STAR)

A **star** is a ball of hot gases that gives off light and other types of energy. (p. 58)

> The twinkling objects in the night sky are great balls of gas and dust called stars.

universe (YŪ-ni-vurs)

The **universe** is everything that exists throughout space. (p. 59)

> The universe is so large that scientists have not yet determined its exact size.

galaxy (GA-luk-sē)

A **galaxy** is a star system that contains large groups of stars. (p. 60)

> This starburst galaxy, M82, is 12 million light-years from Earth.

my Science Vocabulary

dwarf planet (dworf PLA-nit)	planet (PLA-nit)
galaxy (GA-luk-sē)	star (STAR)
moon (MÜN)	universe (YŪ-ni-vurs)

TECHTREK
myNGconnect.com

Vocabulary Games

planet (PLA-nit)

A **planet** is a large nearly round space object that orbits a star. (p. 64)

Venus is one of the eight planets in the solar system.

moon (MÜN)

A **moon** is a large rocky object that orbits a planet. (p. 68)

Earth's moon is covered with craters.

dwarf planet (dworf PLA-nit)

A **dwarf planet** is an object that orbits the sun, is larger than an asteroid and smaller than a planet, and has a nearly round shape. (p. 77)

A dwarf planet is neither a planet nor a satellite.

Stars and Galaxies

Stars What do you see in this clear night sky? Except for the distant glow from city lights, all the light in this night sky comes from stars. A star is a ball of hot gases that gives off light and other types of energy. New stars are born as old ones die. An average star such as our sun will live for billions of years.

The sun is the nearest star to Earth. Like all stars, the sun formed from a huge cloud of dust and gas called a nebula. When stars form, they can grow to many sizes. The smallest ones are the size of planets. The sun is an average-sized star. Still, it's huge. If the sun were a hollow ball, more than a million Earths could fit inside it! The largest stars are many times bigger than the sun. But except for the sun, stars are so far from Earth, they look like points of light.

This view of the night sky is from Arizona.

Stars look close together in the sky. But actually, they are separated by vast distances in space. It's like comparing the distance between the stop sign and the high-wire towers in the picture. The towers look like they are just a little to the left and a little to the right of the stop sign. But you know it would be quite a hike to walk from the sign to one of the towers. Also the distance between the towers is greater than it looks. All three objects look closer to each other than they really are because of your viewpoint.

It's the same thing with stars. They look close together because of our viewpoint from Earth. However, unlike the sign and towers, stars aren't just a kilometer or two apart. Most stars are trillions of kilometers away from each other! Between the stars is some gas and dust but mostly empty space. All of the stars, gas, dust, other objects, and empty space make up the universe . The universe contains everything that exists.

Galaxies Not all of the points of light you see in the night sky are single stars. Powerful telescopes show that some of these points of light are galaxies. A galaxy is a system of stars, gas, and dust held together in space by gravity. Gravity is a force that pulls any two objects toward each other. Many stars have objects moving around, or orbiting, them. Gravity holds these objects in orbit.

The universe contains billions of galaxies in different shapes and sizes. The three main shapes are spiral, elliptical, and irregular.

If you could look down on a spiral galaxy from above, it would look like a pinwheel. Spiral galaxies have a center that is packed with thousands of stars. Moving out from the center are arms that contain many more stars. The arms also contain most of the gas and dust where new stars form.

Stars are forming in the clouds of gas and dust in this irregular galaxy.

TECHTREK
myNGconnect.com

Digital
Library

Find the arms of this spiral galaxy.

Earth is located on an arm of a spiral galaxy called the Milky Way. You can't see the spiral shape because Earth is part of the galaxy. But you can see part of the arm on a clear night. It looks like a white band or pathway across the sky. That is how the Milky Way got its name.

Elliptical galaxies are round or oval with no arms. Elliptical galaxies contain little gas or dust. These materials may have been used up long ago to form the stars in the galaxy.

All other galaxies are called irregular because they have no regular shape. Irregular galaxies contain many clouds of gas and dust in which stars are forming.

Messier 82 (M82) is the name of this elliptical galaxy. The red globs are clouds of hydrogen gas blasting out of the center.

Before You Move On

1. What is a star?
2. What type of galaxy is the Milky Way?
3. **Draw Conclusions** Which type of galaxy is least likely to have many stars forming? Why?

CONSTELLATIONS

Have you ever connected dots on a page to make a picture? The same idea applies to constellations. A constellation is a group of stars that form a recognizable pattern or shape in the sky.

Constellations can be a useful tool. Without modern calendars, ancient peoples relied on star patterns to mark the changes of the seasons. Farmers would decide by constellations when to plant and harvest crops. People also used constellations to explain natural events or religious beliefs. Travelers by land and sea would use the familiar star patterns to find their way around. Even today, stars are used to navigate. In which direction are you looking if you can see Polaris, the north star? You are facing north, of course!

The Big Dipper star pattern is part of a constellation called Ursa Major.

Not every ancient civilization saw the same shape in the sky. The ancient Romans saw a giant man in the grouping of stars known as Orion. Some Native Americans, such as the Lakota, saw a giant hand in the stars that make up Orion's belt. The Dogon people of Africa saw the stars of Orion's belt as a staircase.

Whatever shape is seen, it only looks this way if you are standing on Earth. The constellation appears flat, like words on a page. But if you looked at the stars that make up Orion from space, the shape would be completely different.

Constellations are a human invention. Today, 88 different constellations are recognized by astronomers. The constellations seen in the Northern Hemisphere of Earth are different from those seen in the Southern Hemisphere. In the Northern Hemisphere, most are based on ancient Roman and Greek mythology. In the Southern Hemisphere, the constellations are more modern. They are generally familiar objects or animals, such as a compass or a porpoise.

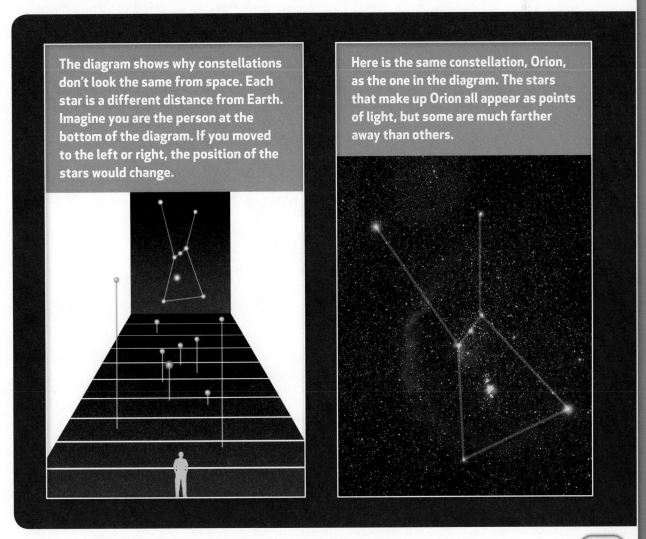

The diagram shows why constellations don't look the same from space. Each star is a different distance from Earth. Imagine you are the person at the bottom of the diagram. If you moved to the left or right, the position of the stars would change.

Here is the same constellation, Orion, as the one in the diagram. The stars that make up Orion all appear as points of light, but some are much farther away than others.

The Solar System

A galaxy is a star system that includes millions of stars. Some star systems, however, have only one star. Within a galaxy, many stars are each at the center of their own star system. One of these star systems is our own solar system. It includes our closest star—the sun—and all the space objects that revolve around it.

Planets are the largest space objects that orbit a star. Our solar system contains eight planets. The diagram shows the order of the planets from the sun. But the distances between the sun and each of the planets are much greater than shown here. Each planet is shaped generally like a ball, but it is not completely spherical, or round. For example, Earth is slightly wider from west to east than it is from north to south. It's like a slightly flattened ball.

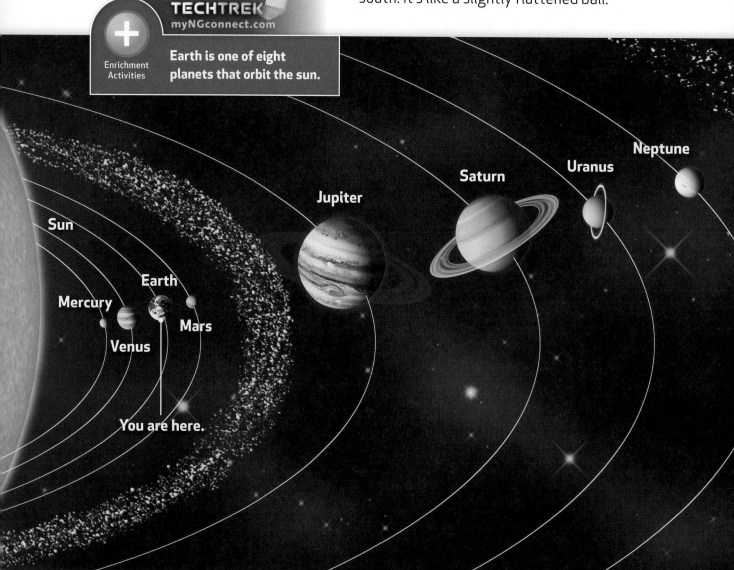

TECHTREK
myNGconnect.com

Enrichment Activities

Earth is one of eight planets that orbit the sun.

Neptune

Uranus

Saturn

Jupiter

Sun

Earth

Mercury

Mars

Venus

You are here.

The eight planets are separated into two groups—the inner planets and the outer planets. The inner planets are closest to the sun. They are made mostly of rock and are also called the rocky planets. Earth is an inner planet.

The outer planets are farthest from the sun. They are made mostly of gases surrounding a smaller rocky core. The outer planets are the largest in the solar system and are also called the gas giants.

Science in a Snap! How Far Apart

Mercury	0.4
Venus	0.7
Earth	1.0
Mars	1.5
Jupiter	5.0
Saturn	9.5
Uranus	19.0
Neptune	30.0

Consider that Earth is 1.0 unit from the sun. The chart shows how many of the same units each of the other planets are from the sun. Choose an object to represent one unit. Use your object to make a scale model.

Make markers labeled Sun and with each planet's name. Use the unit you chose to place the markers on a line.

What do you notice about how far the planets are from one another?

Before You Move On

1. Define what a planet is.
2. How are the inner planets different from the outer planets?
3. **Infer** A year on a planet is how long it takes the planet to orbit the sun once. Why do the planets have years of different lengths?

The Inner Planets

Mercury Mercury is a planet of extremes. It's the smallest and fastest planet and the closest planet to the sun. It has the oldest surface and the wildest temperature changes.

What would it be like on Mercury's surface? The sun would look much bigger than it does from Earth. The landscape would be covered with deep craters caused by space rocks, such as asteroids, crashing into the planet.

Even with a space suit, you would not be able to leave your spacecraft. Mercury has no atmosphere to protect it from the sun's radiation. Also the temperature during the day is extremely hot, and the nights are extremely cold.

TECHTREK
myNGconnect.com

Digital Library

Mercury travels faster than any other planet. It moves 48 kilometers (30 miles) per second around the sun.

MERCURY FACTS

Number of Moons: 0

Length of Rotation: 59 Earth days

Length of Revolution: 88 Earth days

Surface Temperature:
Hottest: about 467°C (870°F)
Coldest: about –183°C (–297°F)

Venus Venus is the second planet from the sun and Earth's closest neighbor. It is almost the same size as Earth, too. When you look into the night sky, only the moon is brighter than Venus.

Venus is probably the last place you would want to land a spacecraft. The atmosphere is made mostly of carbon dioxide. It is extremely thick and poisonous. Lightning, high winds, and difficulty seeing would make landing hard.

Once there, you could not step outside. The pressure of the atmosphere is enormous—strong enough to crush a car! Venus's thick atmosphere also makes it the hottest planet—hot enough to melt lead. This could explain why water doesn't exist on the surface of Venus. Any water would have boiled away.

On Venus the Sun appears to rise toward the west and appears to set toward the east. Can you guess why? Venus rotates in the opposite direction to Earth.

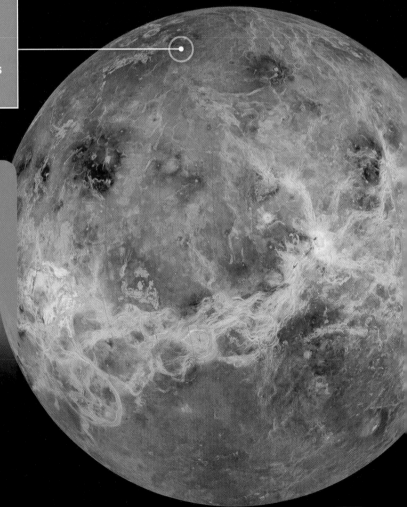

Venus is blanketed in dense clouds of sulfuric acid. This image of Venus's surface was put together using radar waves. The radar waves let astronomers see through the dense clouds.

VENUS FACTS

Number of Moons: 0

Length of Rotation: 243 Earth days

Length of Revolution: 225 Earth days

Surface Temperature:
Average: about 465°C (870°F)

Earth and Its Moon Earth is the third planet from the sun. It is the home of all known life in the universe. Two basic features make life on Earth possible. The first is Earth's distance from the sun. If Earth were closer to the sun, it would be too hot. If Earth were farther away, it would be too cold. The second feature is the presence of liquid water. All living things need water. No other planet has these two features.

Earth's atmosphere is also important to life. The atmosphere is a mixture of gases that surrounds the planet. It extends more than 600 kilometers (about 372 miles) into space. Most of the gases in Earth's atmosphere support, protect, or do no harm to living things.

Earth has one **moon**. A moon is a large rocky object that orbits a planet. Earth's moon has almost no atmosphere. As a result, just about the only time the moon's surface changes is when it gets struck by a rock from space.

With no atmosphere to protect it from space rocks, the moon's surface is covered with craters.

Earth is sometimes called the "blue planet" because most of its surface is covered with water.

EARTH FACTS

Number of Moons: 1

Length of Rotation: 24 hours or 1 day

Length of Revolution: 365 days

Surface Temperature:
Hottest: 58°C (136°F)
Coldest: −88°C (−126°F)

Mars and Its Moons The fourth planet from the sun is Mars. It's only half the size of Earth, but in many ways Mars is more like Earth than any other planet in the solar system is. Mars and Earth both have polar ice caps and four seasons. If you landed on Mars' surface, you would see land features similar to some of the places on Earth's surface. There are canyons, hills, plains, valleys, and volcanoes. In fact, Mars has the largest known volcano in the solar system, Olympus Mons.

If red is your favorite color, then you might like it on Mars. Iron minerals in the soil give the land a rusty-red color.

Since the air on Mars is mostly carbon dioxide, you would need a spacesuit to go exploring. The atmosphere is thinner than Earth's. As a result it is always very cold, especially at night. While you walked around you would see that it is rocky and dry. Your space suit would become very dusty.

In the sky above Mars are Phobos and Deimos, its two tiny moons. Each is only about as wide as a large city. Some scientists think these moons may be asteroids that were caught by the gravity of Mars and pulled into orbit around it.

MARS FACTS

Number of Moons: 2

Length of Rotation: about 1 Earth day

Length of Revolution: 687 Earth days

Surface Temperature:
Hottest: about −30°C (−22°F)
Coldest: about −100°C (−148°F)

There is growing evidence that Mars's surface once held liquid water.

Before You Move On

1. What features of Earth make life possible?
2. Compare and contrast the atmospheres of Venus and Mars.
3. **Infer** Why do you think Mercury takes the least amount of time to travel around the sun?

The Outer Planets

Jupiter and Its Moons The fifth and biggest planet in the solar system is Jupiter. It's the first of the "gas giants." Jupiter is so large that 1,324 Earths could fit inside!

What would it be like if you went to Jupiter? For starters you would have nowhere to land. Jupiter is made of gas. There are no solid surfaces anywhere. Scientists do think Jupiter's core contains some rocky materials. The temperature of the core may be hotter than the surface of the sun.

Even though Jupiter is made of gas, you could not fly a spacecraft into it. The pressure is so great that any solid matter gets crushed.

Jupiter's atmosphere is mostly a mixture of hydrogen and helium gases. Its famous Great Red Spot is a rotating storm, much like a hurricane. It was first discovered more than 300 years ago. Jupiter has a few rings too, but not like the other gas giants. Jupiter's rings are hard to see. They are thought to be the shattered pieces of two moons that smashed into each other.

Jupiter has a huge family of moons. The four largest are about the size of Mercury. Scientists often say that Jupiter is like a solar system all by itself. Each of the moons is different. It's fourth largest, Europa, has a thin shell of ice. But Io, Jupiter's third largest, is covered with active volcanoes and lakes of hot lava.

Jupiter's colorful streaks and bands are super-cooled clouds of water and ammonia.

JUPITER FACTS

Number of Moons: at least 62

Length of Rotation: 9 hours 56 minutes

Length of Revolution: 4,333 Earth days (about 12 Earth years)

Surface Temperature: Average: about –145°C (–229°F)

Saturn and Its Moons The sixth planet, Saturn, is almost twice as far from the sun as Jupiter. It is the second-largest planet in the solar system.

As with all of the gas giants, you would have nowhere to land a spacecraft on Saturn—and you wouldn't want to. Like Jupiter, the pressure in Saturn's clouds would crush anything. The wind would tear a spacecraft apart. Wind speeds in Saturn can reach 500 meters (1,600 feet) per second. That's more than three times faster than the most powerful tornadoes.

Saturn's rings make this planet easy to identify. The rings are made of billions of pieces of ice and rock. Scientists think they are the remains of moons or other objects.

Like Jupiter, Saturn has dozens of moons of many shapes and sizes. Some are located inside its rings. The largest moon, Titan, has an atmosphere.

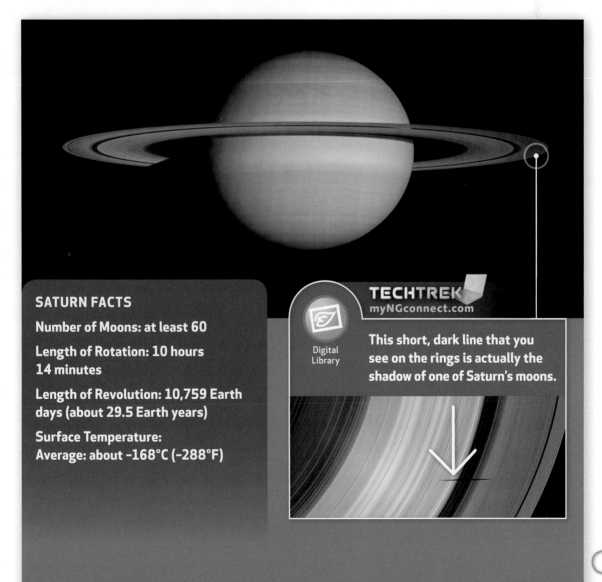

SATURN FACTS

Number of Moons: at least 60

Length of Rotation: 10 hours 14 minutes

Length of Revolution: 10,759 Earth days (about 29.5 Earth years)

Surface Temperature: Average: about –168°C (–288°F)

TECHTREK
myNGconnect.com

Digital Library

This short, dark line that you see on the rings is actually the shadow of one of Saturn's moons.

Uranus and Its Moons The seventh planet from the sun is Uranus. More than four times larger than Earth, Uranus is the third-largest planet in the solar system.

Uranus's atmosphere is mostly hydrogen and helium gases. An outer layer of frozen methane gas surrounds the planet. This gives it its blue-green color. Scientists believe there may be an ocean of liquid water deep within Uranus's atmosphere. But it is unlikely this ocean could support life. Below the ocean is a rocky core about the same size as Earth.

Uranus is tilted on its side. So instead of spinning like a top, it appears to roll like a ball. One idea why is that Uranus was hit by a large space object. The force of the impact tilted the planet.

For decades scientists thought Uranus had only four moons. But when the Voyager 2 spacecraft passed by Uranus in 1986, scientists were excited to find 10 more! Since then, powerful telescopes have helped scientists find even more moons around Uranus. They are difficult to spot from nearly 3 billion kilometers (1.86 million miles) away.

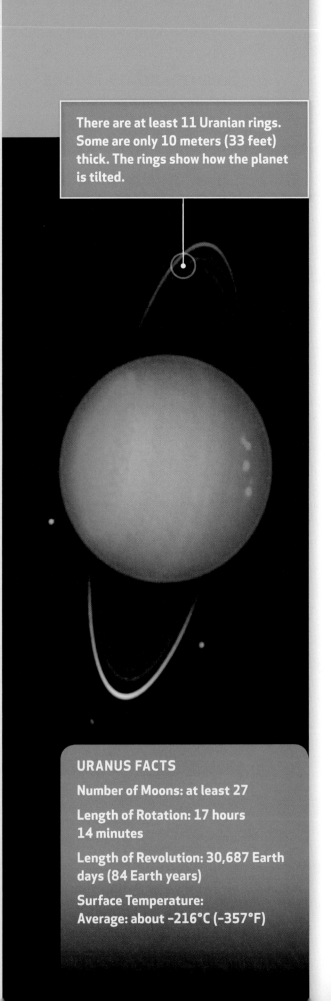

There are at least 11 Uranian rings. Some are only 10 meters (33 feet) thick. The rings show how the planet is tilted.

URANUS FACTS

Number of Moons: at least 27

Length of Rotation: 17 hours 14 minutes

Length of Revolution: 30,687 Earth days (84 Earth years)

Surface Temperature: Average: about −216°C (−357°F)

Neptune and Its Moons

The eighth and last planet in the solar system is Neptune. It is so similar to Uranus that some scientists call them twins. Neptune, like Uranus, has a cold outer layer of methane gas. This gives the planet its blue color. Scientists think there may be an ocean of liquid water in Neptune, too. The water is super-heated, but the pressure in Neptune's atmosphere keeps the water from boiling away.

All of the gas giants are windy, but Neptune's winds are the fastest in the solar system. Winds can blow more than 550 meters (1,800 feet) per second.

Neptune is known to have at least 13 moons. The largest is Triton. It orbits in a direction opposite Neptune's rotation. It is the only moon in the solar system to do this. Scientists think that Triton formed outside of the solar system and was pulled in by Neptune's gravity.

Neptune has a few rings too, but they are very faint. The rings are made of particles of dust.

NEPTUNE FACTS

Number of Moons: at least 13

Length of Rotation: 16 hours 7 minutes

Length of Revolution: 60,190 Earth days (165 Earth years)

Surface Temperature: Average: about –214°C (–353°F)

Before You Move On

1. Describe the atmosphere of Jupiter.
2. Explain how Uranus may have come to be tilted on its side.
3. **Generalize** What are at least four features the gas giants all have in common?

Other Objects in the Solar System

The sun, planets, and moons are not the only objects in the solar system. Other objects include asteroids, dwarf planets, and comets.

Asteroids Asteroids are rocky objects that orbit the sun. They are smaller than dwarf planets. Asteroids range in size from 1,000 kilometers (600 miles) across to as small as a grain of sand. About 50,000 asteroids have been studied so far.

Most asteroids are in the space between Mars and Jupiter. Because it is filled with tens of thousands of asteroids, this area is called the asteroid belt. Scientists have a few ideas about how the asteroid belt formed. Some suggest the asteroids are pieces of a lost planet.

Millions of asteroids travel in a beltway between Mars and Jupiter in this illustration.

About 200 asteroids in the asteroid belt are more than 97 kilometers (60 miles) wide. That's wider than the state of Rhode Island.

Others suggest the asteroids formed when several large objects crashed into each other. A third idea says that they are simply left over material from the formation of the solar system. So far, none of these ideas has been proven or rejected.

Some asteroids travel outside of the main asteroid belt. Their orbits carry them into the area between the orbits of Mars and Earth.

Scientists think some of these asteroids broke away from the asteroid belt. One of the largest of these is Eros. In 2012, this asteroid is expected to pass within 26.7 million kilometers (about 16.6 million miles) of Earth. This is considered to be a very close pass.

The asteroid Eros is about 34 kilometers long. In 2001 a spacecraft orbited the asteroid and then landed on it. The spacecraft sent back information to Earth.

Dwarf Planets

From 1930 until 2006, the solar system had a ninth planet called Pluto. Then in 2006, an international meeting of scientists changed the definition of a planet. Pluto had to be reclassified.

Recall that a planet is the largest type of nearly round space object to orbit a star. Other than the sun itself, the eight planets are the largest objects in the solar system. But Pluto is much smaller than Mercury, and smaller than our moon. Most scientists agree that Pluto is not large enough to be a planet.

Since Pluto's discovery in 1930, it has traveled only one-third of its way around the sun.

Pluto and its three moons Charon, Nix, and Hydra. Charon is nearly the same size as Pluto.

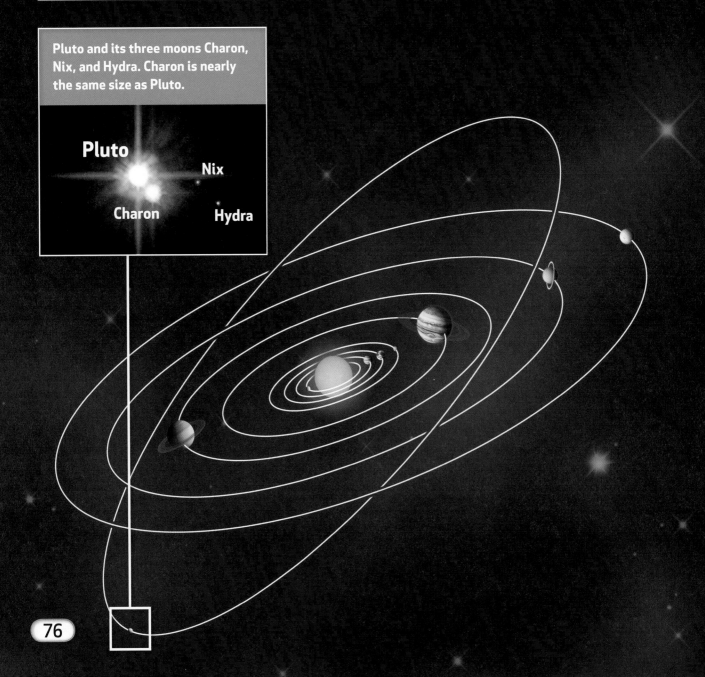

Pluto

Nix

Charon

Hydra

Pluto's size makes it a **dwarf planet.** A dwarf planet is an object that orbits the sun, is larger than an asteroid and smaller than a planet, and has a nearly round shape. Our solar system has five known dwarf planets.

Pluto is mainly ice. It has a thin atmosphere, mostly of methane gas. Pluto is also extremely cold. If you could stand on Pluto's surface, the sun would look dim and small because it is so far away.

Compared with the planets, Pluto's orbit is unusual. It moves at an angle to the eight planets. At certain times Pluto crosses inside Neptune's orbit.

One dwarf planet, Ceres, used to be considered a large asteroid. It travels in the asteroid belt and shares its orbit with thousands of asteroids. But in 2006, scientists decided it was actually a dwarf planet. Ceres is about 950 kilometers (590 miles) wide—wider than Nevada. Ceres's size means it is large enough to have strong gravity. Its stronger gravity holds it in the shape of a sphere. For these reasons, Ceres was classified as a dwarf planet.

TECHTREK
myNGconnect.com

Digital Library

This photo shows that Ceres's shape is nearly spherical.

Comets One of the more unusual objects in space is a comet. Imagine a ball of ice and rock flying through space. That is basically a comet. When comets pass close to the sun, the sun's energy changes some of the ice to gas. The comet begins to glow. The glowing part is called a coma. A trail of gas and dust streams out behind it. The stream is called a tail. The tail can extend for millions of miles into space! Eventually, the comet travels far enough from the sun that it refreezes. The comet stays frozen until the next time it passes close to the sun.

Comets leave behind a trail of rocky dust. Planets often pass through these trails. On Earth, passing through the trail left by a comet makes one of the most amazing sights in the night sky. These are meteor showers, also known as shooting stars. Meteor showers are thousands of bits of solid material hitting Earth's atmosphere and burning up. Every year, Earth passes through the remains of at least 12 comets.

Comets orbit the sun in an area beyond Neptune called the Kuiper (kī'pur) belt. Some comets have short orbits. They return close to Earth often enough to be recorded in history. Halley's Comet returns every 76 years.

As the glowing comet continues its orbit around the sun, the tail points away from the sun.

Pieces of asteroids or comets that fall through space and enter Earth's atmosphere are called meteoroids. Meteoroids are smaller than comets and asteroids. Friction between a meteoroid and Earth's atmosphere causes heat first, then light. The light you see streaking across the sky is a meteor, or shooting star.

If an asteroid, comet, or meteoroid does not burn up completely on its trip through the atmosphere, it can land on Earth's surface. These pieces of space rock are called meteorites.

This meteor shower was caused by the comet Tempel-Tuttle.

This meteorite found in Saudi Arabia weighs more than a medium-sized car!

Before You Move On

1. Describe how asteroids might have formed.
2. Explain what happens as a comet's orbit brings it closer to the sun.
3. **Evaluate** Do you think the decision to classify Pluto as a dwarf planet was correct or incorrect? Explain your reasoning.

Conclusion

The solar system is within the Milky Way Galaxy. It is one of countless star systems throughout the universe. The sun and everything else in the solar system formed within a nebula billions of years ago. This includes the eight planets, a few dwarf planets, and many moons, asteroids, and comets.

Big Idea Our solar system is made up of everything that revolves around the sun, including planets, dwarf planets, moons, asteroids, and comets.

THE SUN + PLANETS AND MOONS + DWARF PLANETS, ASTEROIDS, AND COMETS = THE SOLAR SYSTEM

Vocabulary Review

Match the following terms with the correct definition.

A. galaxy

B. planet

C. moon

D. universe

E. star

F. dwarf planet

1. Everything that exists throughout space
2. A star system that contains large groups of stars
3. A gaseous sphere that gives off light and other types of energy
4. A large, round, rocky object that orbits a planet
5. An object that orbits the sun, is larger than an asteroid and smaller than a planet, and has a nearly round shape
6. A large nearly round space object that orbits a star

Big Idea Review

1. **List** List the eight planets in order from the sun.

2. **Describe** Identify and describe one gas giant other than Jupiter.

3. **Compare and contrast** Explain how the inner and outer planets are alike and different.

4. **Interpret** Why is the sun considered to be an average star?

5. **Infer** We can't see the spiral shape of our galaxy. How is this like not being able to see the shape of a forest you are in?

6. **Draw Conclusions** Some scientists like to say that Jupiter is almost a solar system all by itself. Why isn't Jupiter a solar system?

Write About the Solar System

Explain This is a photo of Mercury's surface. What features can you identify? Why does the surface look like this?

CHAPTER 2 EARTH SCIENCE EXPERT: GEOLOGIST

Do you want to know about space rocks? Ask a geologist who studies meteorites.

Have you ever wished on a shooting star? Do you wonder if they ever land on Earth? We might not all get to space someday, but many of us could have the opportunity to study objects that come from beyond the solar system. Dr. Meenakshi Wadhwa from Arizona State University is just the person to ask about space rocks. She is in charge of a huge collection of meteorites—over 1,550 of them.

What do you do?

I teach students at a university and conduct research about rocks from space. I am also in charge of the Center for Meteorite Studies. Our center contains the largest meteorite collection at a university in the world.

Do you see a strong connection between what you do and Earth science?

There is a very strong connection! The basic ideas of Earth science form the foundation of my research. My scientific work involves studying rocks from other places in our solar system, such as meteorites and moon rocks. I also apply a lot of ideas from other physical sciences, such as physics and chemistry.

What would you say has been the coolest part of your job?

I would say that would be getting to interact with students who are really excited to learn and helping them make new discoveries.

TECHTREK
myNGconnect.com

Student
eEdition

Digital
Library

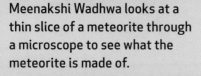

Meenakshi Wadhwa looks at a thin slice of a meteorite through a microscope to see what the meteorite is made of.

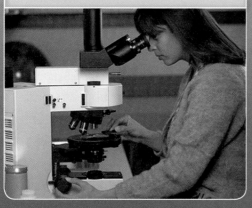

A smooth slice through a meteorite shows the different kinds of rocky material that make it up

What has been your greatest accomplishment so far?

One accomplishment has been in my scientific research. My work has helped advance our understanding about the timing of the formation of our solar system. Another accomplishment has been to motivate some of my students to go into careers in the sciences and in science education.

What did you like about science in elementary school?

When I was young, I had questions about everything, and science in school allowed me to understand the natural world around me. I didn't have a specific view of where I would end up. But I did know that I would be doing something fun, where I would get to apply my interest in the sciences.

What did you study in school and in college? Did you continue to study after college?

In school I studied a variety of subjects, including languages, geography, and the basic sciences. In college I majored in geology and had minors in physics and chemistry. After college, I went to graduate school and earned a doctorate (PhD) in Earth and Planetary Sciences.

Wadhwa examines one of the many large meteorites from the meteorite vault at Arizona State University.

BECOME AN EXPERT

Asteroids and Comets: Friends or Foes?

Asteroids and comets have been crashing into **planets** ever since the sun and planets were born billions of years ago. All you need to do is look at Mercury or Mars to see the scars left by such impacts. The surface of Earth's **moon** is largely shaped by these impacts. What about Earth? Are we safe from these events? Not exactly.

About 5,000 years ago in Australia, a giant asteroid or comet broke up over the sky. Its huge pieces fell like bombs, exploding into Earth's surface. What is left today is a cluster of 13 craters. Events like this one have happened many times in Earth's long history.

The famous Barringer Meteor Crater in Arizona is about 1,219 meters (4,000 feet) wide and 168 meters (550 feet) deep.

planet
A **planet** is a large nearly round space object that orbits a star.

moon
A **moon** is a large object that orbits a planet.

TECHTREK
myNGconnect.com

Student
eEdition

Digital
Library

Craters are dents in the ground caused by the force of a meteor's or comet's impact. More than 200 craters have been found on Earth so far. Why so few compared to the thousands of craters on the moon? Unlike the moon, Earth has an atmosphere. Most space rocks that would strike Earth burn up as they rub against the gas particles in the atmosphere. Some asteroids or comets have been large enough to make it through the atmosphere and form craters. But most craters have been worn away by weathering and erosion.

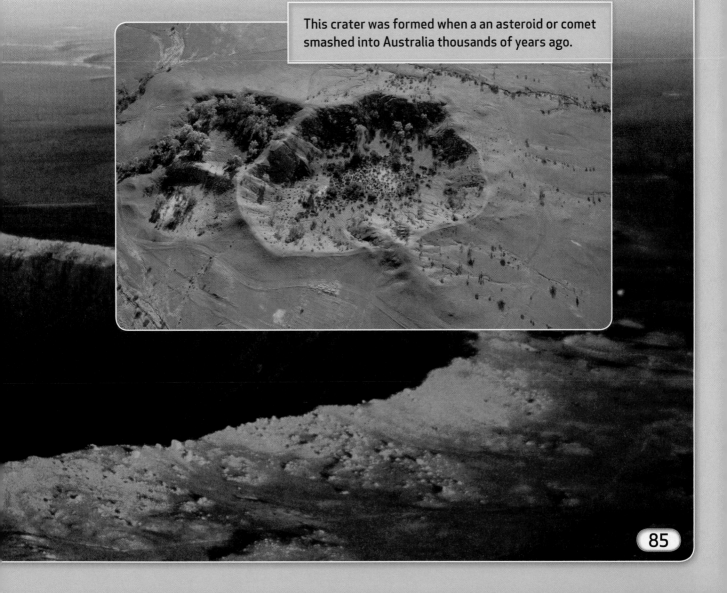

This crater was formed when a an asteroid or comet smashed into Australia thousands of years ago.

Rocks in Space Billions of asteroids and comets speed through the Milky Way Galaxy . Most comets orbit the sun near the outer edge of the solar system. Most asteroids orbit the sun between Mars and Jupiter. Scientists once thought Ceres was the largest asteroid. They now think it is big enough to be a **dwarf planet** .

Even though there are millions of asteroids in the asteroid belt, they are spread apart. If they were gathered together to form one large asteroid, it would still be smaller than the moon.

This illustration shows Ceres's nearly round shape. Some astronomers think there could be frozen water below its rocky surface.

galaxy
A **galaxy** is a star system that contains large groups of stars.

dwarf planet
A **dwarf planet** is an object that orbits the sun, is larger than an asteroid and smaller than a planet, and has a nearly round shape.

In 2001, a spacecraft called NEAR (Near Earth Asteroid Rendezvous) landed on one of the largest known asteroids, Eros. This was the first time a spacecraft orbited and landed on an asteroid. NEAR was able to take and send back to Earth 69 pictures of Eros before the spacecraft stopped working. The photos show that Eros has long grooves and many craters.

TECHTREK
myNGconnect.com

Digital Library

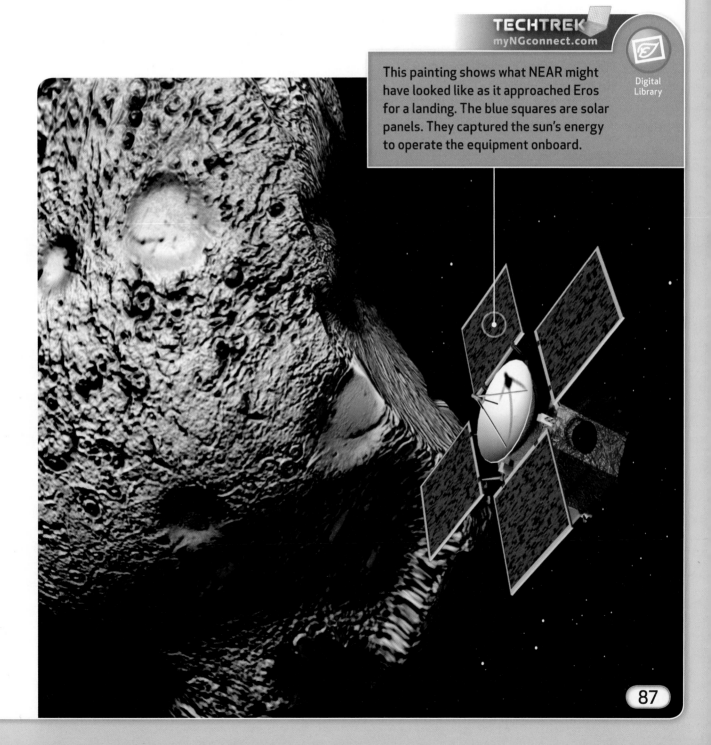

This painting shows what NEAR might have looked like as it approached Eros for a landing. The blue squares are solar panels. They captured the sun's energy to operate the equipment onboard.

Near Earth Objects Most asteroids in the asteroid belt are not a threat to Earth. They stay in the belt for the most part. Some, however, do drift out of the asteroid belt and come closer to Earth.

Asteroids that come close to Earth are called Near-Earth Objects. The asteroid Apophis is an example of a Near Earth Object.

It was discovered just a few years ago, and already scientists are watching it closely. Apophis is 320 meters (1,050 feet) wide. It passes Earth about every 16 years. With each pass, Apophis gets a little closer to Earth. In 2029, it will be only 35,000 kilometers (22,000 miles) away.

THE SKY IS FALLING

Scientists think a large asteroid or comet hit Earth about 65 million years ago. These paintings show what might have happened.

All was peaceful a few seconds before the crash.

The asteroid or comet streaks through Earth's atmosphere. Part of it burns up.

This may seem like a safe distance, but it's close enough that Earth's gravity might change the asteroid's orbit. That could be a big problem. Instead of passing by Earth, this asteroid could eventually slam into Earth.

Today an entire program at NASA, the Near Earth Object program, is dedicated to identifying and tracking Near Earth Objects.

This crater in western Australia was formed about 300,000 years ago. It's 880 meters (2,887 feet) across. It used to be twice as deep, but windblown sand has filled it in.

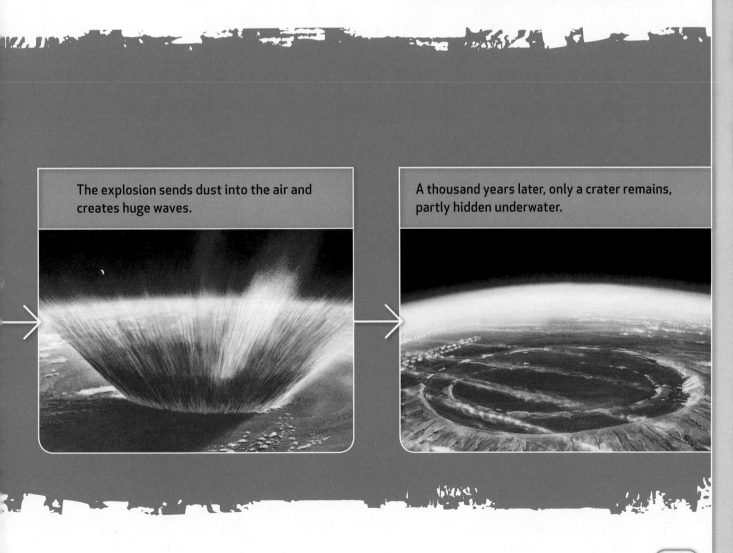

The explosion sends dust into the air and creates huge waves.

A thousand years later, only a crater remains, partly hidden underwater.

Taking Action In order to learn more about Apophis and the possibility of it impacting Earth, NASA plans to send a spacecraft to the asteroid. The spacecraft would put a homing beacon on the asteroid so that scientists could track it.

Chances are Apophis will never slam into Earth. But just in case, scientists are working on a plan. First, they want to chart Apophis's path through space. Then, they want to send another spacecraft there to collect data. The data will help them plan what to do next.

Scientists might use what they know about gravity to pull the asteroid out of its orbit. One idea is to send a special spacecraft to the asteroid. The spacecraft and its gravity would act like a tractor and pull the asteroid into a new path away from Earth.

Using powerful telescopes, scientists have discovered asteroid belts orbiting distant stars. Asteroids and comets are just a few of the many amazing objects in the universe. They are worth watching in more ways than one.

How do you move an asteroid? This painting shows how the spacecraft's gravity might pull the asteroid to a new position.

universe

The **universe** is everything that exists throughout space.

star

A **star** is a ball of hot gases that gives off light and other types of energy.

CHAPTER
2

SHARE AND COMPARE

Turn and Talk Why is it important to track the paths of asteroids and comets? Form a complete answer to this question together with a partner.

Read Select two pages in this section. Practice reading the pages. Then read them aloud to a partner. Talk about why the pages are interesting.

my SCIENCE notebook

Write Write a conclusion that tells the important ideas about what you have learned about asteroids and comets hitting Earth. State what you think is the Big Idea of this section. Share what you wrote with a classmate. Compare your conclusions. Did your classmate recall what happens to most asteroids that enter Earth's atmosphere?

my SCIENCE notebook

Draw Look again at the Barringer Meteor Crater at the beginning of this section. Work in small groups. Draw what might have happened to make this crater. Have each person in the group draw one step in the process of how this crater formed. Compare your drawings with other groups.

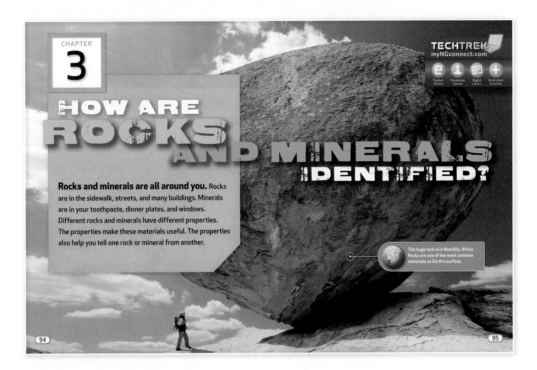

CHAPTER 3

HOW ARE ROCKS AND MINERALS IDENTIFIED?

Rocks and minerals are all around you. Rocks are in the sidewalk, streets, and many buildings. Minerals are in your toothpaste, dinner plates, and windows. Different rocks and minerals have different properties. The properties make these materials useful. The properties also help you tell one rock or mineral from another.

TECHTREK
myNGconnect.com

The huge rock is in Namibia, Africa. Rocks are one of the most common materials on Earth's surface.

After reading Chapter 3, you will be able to:

- Explain that rocks and soils are made of minerals. **MINERALS, MINERALS IN ROCKS AND SOIL**

- Identify the physical properties of minerals. **PROPERTIES OF MINERALS**

- Explain that rocks are classified according to their formation. **CLASSIFYING ROCKS**

- Identify and explain the processes involved in the rock cycle **THE ROCK CYCLE**

- **Science in a Snap!** Explain that rocks are classified according to their formation. **CLASSIFYING ROCKS**

HOW ARE ROCKS AND

Rocks and minerals are all around you. Rocks are in the sidewalk, streets, and many buildings. Minerals are in your toothpaste, dinner plates, and windows. Different rocks and minerals have different properties. The properties make these materials useful. The properties also help you tell one rock or mineral from another.

TECHTREK
myNGconnect.com

Student
eEdition

Vocabulary
Games

Digital
Library

Enrichment
Activities

MINERALS
IDENTIFIED?

The huge rock is in Namibia, Africa.
Rocks are one of the most common
materials on Earth's surface.

95

SCIENCE VOCABULARY

crystal (KRIHS-tuhl)

A **crystal** is a solid that has atoms arranged in a repeating pattern. (p. 98)

The mineral, emerald, has long crystals.

atom (AT-uhm)

An **atom** is the smallest piece of matter that can still be identified as that matter. (p. 98)

Sulphur is a pure substance as it is made of only one type of atom.

igneous (IG-nē-us)

Igneous rock forms when melted rock cools and becomes solid. (p. 106)

Igneous rocks such as granite are often used as building materials for walls and floors.

my Science Vocabulary

atom	metamorphic
(AT-uhm)	(met-a-MOR-fik)
crystal	**rock cycle**
(KRIHS-tuhl)	(ROK SĪ-kuhl)
igneous	**sedimentary**
(IG-nē-us)	(sed-i-MEN-tah-rē)

TECHTREK
myNGconnect.com

Vocabulary Games

sedimentary
(sed-i-MEN-tah-rē)

Sedimentary rock forms from small pieces of rocks and minerals that are cemented together. (p. 108)

> Pieces of rock and minerals were cemented together to form this sedimentary rock.

metamorphic
(met-a-MOR-fik rok)

Metamorphic rock forms from rock that has been changed by high temperature, high pressure, and hot liquids and gases. (p. 112)

> Metamorphic rocks often have wavy bands of light and dark minerals.

rock cycle (ROK SĪ-kuhl)

The **rock cycle** is a series of actions that changes rocks from one type to another. (p. 115)

> The melted rock, called lava, will harden into solid rock as part of the rock cycle.

Minerals

Look around you. What materials do you see on Earth's surface? The most common are rocks and soil. Rocks and soil are made of minerals. A mineral is a solid, nonliving material that forms in nature. All minerals have the following five characteristics.

Natural A mineral forms in nature on or below Earth's surface. Minerals made by scientists in laboratories are not true minerals.

Crystal Structure Minerals, like all matter, are made up of atoms. An atom is the smallest piece of matter. The atoms in minerals are arranged in crystals. A crystal forms when atoms are arranged in a pattern that repeats. Different minerals have different crystal shapes.

Chemical Makeup A pure substance made of only one kind of atom is called an element. Some minerals, like sulphur, are made of one element. Other minerals are made of two or more elements joined together. Rock salt is made of the elements called sodium and chloride.

Emerald

Rock Salt

Sulphur

Solid Minerals are solids. Crystals are only present in solids.

Nonliving A mineral is not a living thing and is not made from living things. For example plants and animals are not minerals because they are living.

Identifying minerals can sometimes be confusing. You may not think of ice as a mineral. But lets apply our five characteristics. Ice is natural, it is a solid, it has a crystal structure, it is nonliving, and it is made of elements. Therefore it is a mineral. Water, however is not a mineral. It does not fit the five characteristics. Can you tell why?

Ice crystals have formed on this window.

Before You Move On

1. What are the five characteristics of minerals?
2. How are atoms and crystals related?
3. **Apply** Diamonds that are mined from the ground are minerals. Some diamonds are made in a laboratory with the same characteristics as a natural diamond. Is the human-made diamond a mineral? Explain.

Properties of Minerals

Scientists have identified about 4,000 different kinds of minerals. How can you tell them apart? Minerals are classified by their properties. To identify a mineral, you compare its properties to the properties of known minerals.

Luster   Luster is how the surface of a mineral reflects light. A mineral's luster is either metallic or nonmetallic. A metallic luster reflects light like some metals. A nonmetallic luster does not reflect light.

Crystal Shape   You can use crystal shape to help identify some minerals. Crystals might be shaped like cubes or shoe boxes or have other shapes. The same kind of mineral has the same crystal shape.

Hardness   The measure of how easily a mineral is scratched is hardness. Scientists use a scale called the Mohs scale to find a mineral's hardness. A soft mineral that is easily scratched with a fingernail has a hardness of 1. The hardest mineral is diamond. It has a hardness of 10 and can scratch all other minerals.

This mineral is a type of quartz called amethyst. It has a glassy luster.

Streak A mineral's streak is the color of powder a mineral leaves when rubbed on an unglazed piece of tile. The tile is called a streak plate. The mineral will leave a streak only if it is softer than the streak plate. If the mineral is harder than the streak plate, it will scratch the plate instead.

Look at the streak of hematite below. The mineral is blue-gray, but it leaves a red-brown streak. A mineral's streak is often a different color than the mineral. Also, the same mineral can be different colors. Hematite can be gray, black, brown, red, or blue-gray. But the streak is always the same color.

The mineral quartz is hard enough to scratch glass.

The streak of hematite is always red-brown no matter what color the hematite.

Cleavage Some minerals have flat surfaces called cleavage planes, like the feldspar shown below. If a mineral breaks, or cleaves, along these surfaces, it has cleavage. Some minerals have only one cleavage plane. They break into flat sheets. Minerals shaped like cubes have three cleavage planes. Many minerals do not cleave at all.

Color A few minerals are always the same color. For example, malachite is always green. Azurite is always blue. But most minerals can be more than one color. For example, quartz can be white, pink, yellow, purple, brown, gray, or clear. Scientists use color in combination with the other properties of minerals to identify them.

Feldspar has two cleavage planes.

These mineral samples are all different colors. Yet they are all the same mineral—fluorite.

Common Minerals

Although there are about 4,000 different minerals, they do not occur in equal amounts. Only about 30 different minerals are common. These minerals form most of the rocks in Earth's crust. The chart lists a few of these common minerals. Compare their properties. Notice that some minerals have the same properties. But no two minerals have the exact same set of properties.

TECHTREK
myNGconnect.com

Enrichment Activities

COMMON **MINERALS**

Mineral Name	Hardness	Streak	Cleavage Planes	Common Color	
BIOTITE MICA	2–3	white	1	brown/black	
CALCITE	3	white	3	white	
DOLOMITE	4	white	3	white/gray	
FELDSPAR	6–6.5	white	2	white or pink	
HORNBLENDE	5–6	white	2	black	
MUSCOVITE MICA	2–3	white	1	white	
OLIVINE	6.5–7	white	1	green	
PYROXENE	5–6.5	white	2	green/black	
QUARTZ	7	white	none	white, pink, gray, clear	

Before You Move On

1. What is a mineral's streak?
2. Why should several properties be used to identify a mineral?
3. **Apply** Mineral A scratches mineral B. Mineral A is scratched by mineral C. List the minerals in order from softest to hardest.

Minerals in Rocks and Soil

Rocks Now that you know what minerals are, you might wonder what the difference is between minerals and rocks. Rocks are natural solids made up of materials from Earth's crust. Most of these materials are minerals. So almost all rocks are made of minerals.

Some rocks are made of hard materials that are not minerals. These materials do not have all five characteristics of minerals. For example, the material that makes up the rock obsidian does not have crystals. So obsidian is a rock but it is not made of minerals.

Some rocks are made of only one mineral. For example, rock salt is made up of the mineral halite. Most rocks, however, are made up of two or more minerals. Sandstone is a rock that is made up of mostly two minerals—feldspar and quartz. Granite is also made of feldspar and quartz but it contains other minerals, such as mica and hornblende.

The different colors in this sandstone are caused by different minerals.

Soil Soil also contains minerals. Soil begins to form when rocks break down into smaller and smaller pieces. Over time, loose pieces of rocks and minerals mix with bits of dead plants and animals, water, and air. This mixture of matter is soil.

If you could look at a handful of the soil shown in the picture, what would you see? You might see some pebbles and larger stones. You also might see and feel tiny bits of sand. Each grain of sand is a piece of rock or mineral.

Soil is used for growing crops. It's also important for construction. Most homes and roads are not built directly on rock. They are built on top of and in the soil.

Before You Move On

1. What is a rock?
2. How are rocks, soil, and minerals related?
3. **Infer** Not all soils look the same. Why do you think some soils in different parts of the country are different colors?

Classifying Rocks

You may think rocks are all the same, but observe the rocks on these next few pages. Each is different. Scientists classify rocks into three types based on how they formed.

Igneous Rock The granite and obsidian shown below are two examples of `igneous rocks`. The word *igneous* means "fire." Igneous rocks form from melted rock, either on Earth's surface or below it.

As melted rock cools, it becomes solid. Crystals of minerals form. The crystals lock together like pieces of a jigsaw puzzle.

Observe the granite below. Notice how the individual crystals are linked. How many different minerals can you see? The minerals shown are quartz, feldspar, and mica.

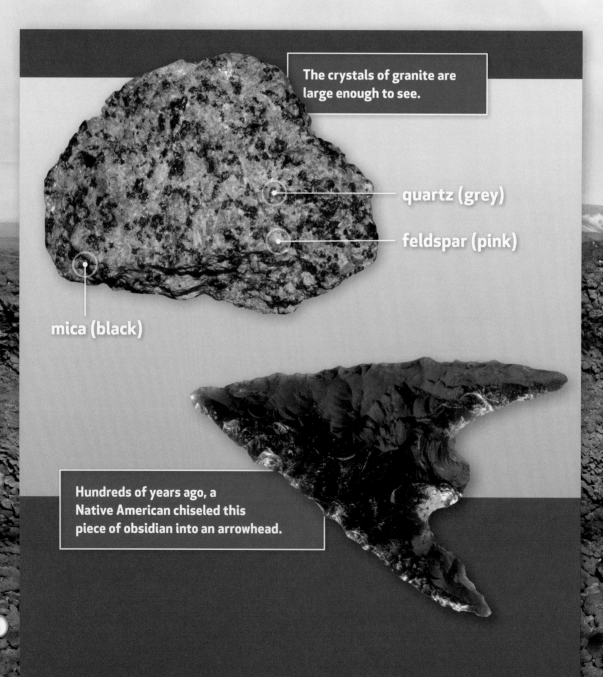

The crystals of granite are large enough to see.

quartz (grey)

feldspar (pink)

mica (black)

Hundreds of years ago, a Native American chiseled this piece of obsidian into an arrowhead.

You can see the different minerals in the granite because the crystals are large. The size of the crystals depends on how quickly the melted rock cooled. Larger crystals grow when the rock cools slowly underground. That's where most igneous rock forms.

Melted rock cools quickly when it erupts onto the surface, such as from a volcano. Melted rock on the surface is called lava. Sometimes it cools so quickly that no crystals form. Obsidian forms this way.

The cliffs shown below are made of basalt. This igneous rock formed as lava poured from huge cracks in the ground about 10 million years ago. The lava cooled quickly. The crystals are too small to see.

What you can see in the basalt are lots of holes. These holes formed as gas bubbles escaped from the lava. As the lava cooled and the rock became solid, the holes remained.

You can see the holes formed by escaping gas in this close-up photo.

These basalt cliffs form part of the coast of Iceland, Europe.

Sedimentary Rock

The rocks shown below are examples of **sedimentary** rocks. Sedimentary rocks form from small pieces of rock and minerals that get cemented together. These pieces are called sediments.

Most sediment forms from weathering or the breaking of rock into smaller and smaller pieces. Mud in a field, sand on a beach, and pebbles in a creek are examples of sediment.

Then erosion moves the sediment to a new place. Eventually the sediment comes to rest. Over millions of years, thick layers of sediments build up on the ocean floor, at the bottom of rivers, and on dry land.

To understand what happens next, think about squeezing a fistful of mud. The pressure squeezes the mud particles together. A handful of loose sediment becomes a tighter, harder clump. The same kind of action helps form many sedimentary rocks.

This sedimentary rock is sandstone. It formed almost 200 million years ago from sand dunes that were squeezed by thick layers of sand above it.

Top layers of sediments press down on bottom layers. This weight squeezes sediments on the bottom layers together, just like your fistful of mud, except a lot tighter.

But something else happens in the sediment layers that doesn't happen to the mud in your hand. Water trickles through the spaces between the pieces of sediment. Minerals that are dissolved in the water act like glue between the pieces of sediment. When the sediments become cemented together, sedimentary rock forms.

Many sedimentary rocks have layers, such as the ones shown here. Each layer represents a time when sediments were brought into the area and laid down.

SEDIMENT TO ROCK

MUD	+	PRESSURE AND CEMENTING	=	SHALE
SAND	+	PRESSURE AND CEMENTING	=	SANDSTONE
PEBBLES	+	PRESSURE AND CEMENTING	=	CONGLOMERATE

Fossils Some sedimentary rocks contain the traces of plants and animals such as shells, bones, leaf prints, and even footprints. These traces are called fossils. When organisms die, their remains may become buried in sediments. Eventually, the sediments are cemented together, and sedimentary rock forms. Soft parts, such as flesh, usually decay. Hard parts, such as shells, may not decay and eventually leave an impression in the rock.

What can you learn about the past by observing this fossil footprint?

The shape of ocean animals called trilobites that lived millions of years ago is preserved as a fossil in rock.

HOW SOME **FOSSILS FORM**

Long ago, many trilobites died and settled to the bottom of the ocean.

→

Sediment buried the trilobites and became sedimentary rock.

→

Minerals dissolved in water replaced minerals in the trilobite skeletons, forming fossils.

Scientists study fossils to learn about the climate and environment in which the organisms lived. Observe the rocks below. Why do you think they look like tree logs?

These rocks are parts of tree fossils. The trees lived about 225 million years ago. From studying the rock around the fossils, scientists know that a volcanic eruption knocked the trees down. The trees were buried in ash and lava. More eruptions built up more layers of ash and lava. Deep underground, minerals dissolved in water slowly replaced the wood. Over millions of years, the logs of wood became logs of rock, or petrified wood.

These fossil trees are in the Petrified Forest National Park in Arizona. Today, trees that are similar to these fossils live in areas that are wet and warm. So these fossil trees are a clue that Arizona once had a wet and warm climate.

These fossil trees are well-preserved. You can see the shape of the tree bark and even count the tree rings!

Metamorphic Rock

Observe the rock below. The wavy bands make it look like great forces bent and twisted the rock. That's exactly what happened. This rock, called gneiss (NĪS), is a kind of **metamorphic rock** . Metamorphic rocks form when heat or pressure, or both, change rocks. In fact, the word metamorphic means "change form."

Rocks don't melt as they become metamorphic. The minerals and crystal shape in the rocks change, but the rocks stay solid. Sometimes the crystals line up and form stripes, or bands. This is banded metamorphic rock. The gneiss shown here is an example. A common non-banded metamorphic rock is marble. It forms from limestone.

This rock used to be granite. Extreme heat and pressure underground turned it into gneiss. Is this rock banded or not banded?

Rocks can change when they are heated. This happens in different ways. Melted rock underground, or magma, might rise through cracks in Earth's crust. As the magma touches cooler solid rock, the rock gets hot. It may change to metamorphic rock. Rocks also get hot as huge sections of crust get pushed down below the surface. The heat increases with greater depth.

Pressure also increases. As rocks are pushed deeper under the Earth's surface, rocks on top push down on rocks below. The lower rocks are squeezed, bent, and twisted.

Over time, these metamorphic rocks may be pushed up to Earth's surface, such as the gneiss in the photo.

Science in a Snap! Changes in Rocks

This picture shows a sedimentary rock made of pebbles cemented together. Observe it carefully.

This picture shows the same kind of rock, but it has changed and become a metamorphic rock. Compare the two rocks.

How are the two rocks the same? How are they different? What caused the changes?

Before You Move On

1. Explain why igneous rocks have crystals of different sizes.
2. How do the three major types of rocks form?
3. **Draw Conclusions** Why aren't fossils found in metamorphic rock?

The Rock Cycle

The different kinds of rocks that you have read about are always changing. On Earth's surface, wind, water, and ice break up rocks and move them from place to place. Some rocks are pushed deep underground. Heat and pressure bend, twist, and melt the rocks. Melted rock often erupts onto the surface, such as the lava shown below. Eruptions like this happen on the ocean floor too.

These processes slowly change rocks from one type to another. The three main types of rocks often form and then reform into another type. Because rocks are always changing, not even the oldest rocks on Earth are the original rocks of the crust. Earth's rocks have changed many times throughout its long history.

This lava is cooling into solid igneous rock. The moment this rock forms, wind and water start breaking it apart.

The series of changes from one type of rock to another is called the rock cycle . Notice in the diagram that any type of rock can change into any other type of rock.

Use your finger to trace a pathway through the rock cycle. What processes did your pathway include? Most of these processes take millions of years to happen.

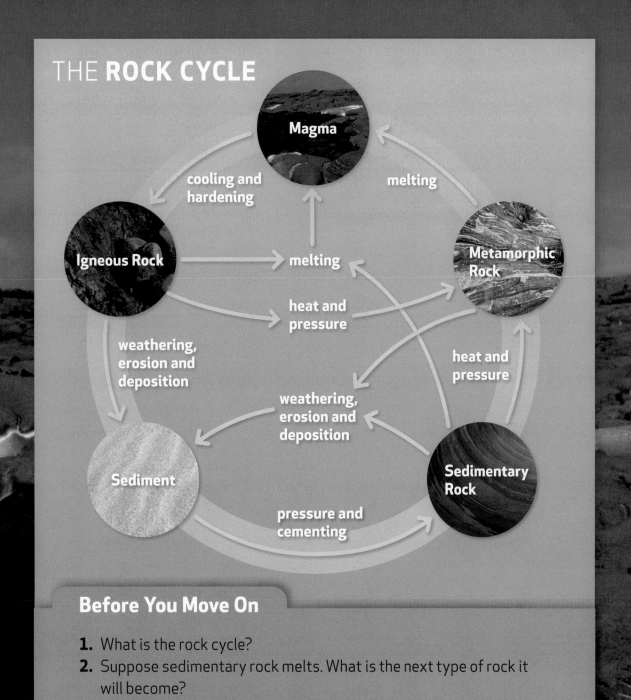

THE ROCK CYCLE

Magma

melting

cooling and hardening

Igneous Rock

melting

Metamorphic Rock

heat and pressure

weathering, erosion and deposition

heat and pressure

weathering, erosion and deposition

Sediment

Sedimentary Rock

pressure and cementing

Before You Move On

1. What is the rock cycle?
2. Suppose sedimentary rock melts. What is the next type of rock it will become?
3. **Interpret Diagrams** Describe a pathway through the rock cycle that does not include all three rock types.

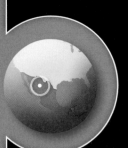

NATIONAL GEOGRAPHIC

THE AMAZING CAVE OF CRYSTALS

One of the best places to find interesting rocks and minerals is a cave. Just ask the people exploring the cave shown here near Chihuahua, Mexico. In April, 2000, workers in a lead and silver mine broke through a wall of rock and discovered what became known as the Cave of Crystals. What they found looked like something from a science fiction movie. They had discovered the largest known crystals of any kind, anywhere in the world!

Some of the giant crystals are as thick and tall as telephone poles. The largest ones are over 11 meters (36 feet) tall!

These crystals are as big as telephone poles.

The crystals in this cave are of the mineral gypsum. Crushed gypsum makes up wallboard and sidewalk chalk. But here is how gypsum looks if it has the space and time to grow into its full crystal shape.

Before the nearby mines had been dug, this cave was full of water. Chemicals that were dissolved in the water slowly grew into crystals.

Scientists think the crystals grew bit by bit for about 600,000 years. When the surrounding area was drained for the mines, water drained from the cave, too. The crystals stopped growing. But now they are available to see and explore.

To explore this cave, you have to go 300 meters (1,000 feet) underground.

This group of gypsum crystals is about the size of a football. That's small compared to most of the giant crystals in the cave.

Earth's materials include minerals, rocks, and soil. Rocks and minerals are two main ingredients of soil. Minerals can be identified by their properties because each mineral has its own set of properties. Rocks are classified by how they form. The three main types of rocks are igneous, sedimentary, and metamorphic. Rocks slowly but constantly change from one type to another in the rock cycle.

Big Idea Minerals are identified based on their properties such as hardness, luster, streak, cleavage, and color. Rocks are identified and classified based on how they form.

MINERALS IN ROCKS AND SOIL

Rocks   Minerals   Soil

Vocabulary Review

Match the following terms with the correct definition.

A. crystal
B. sedimentary
C. rock cycle
D. metamorphic
E. igneous
F. atom

1. The smallest piece of matter that can still be identified as that matter
2. Type of rock that forms when melted rock cools and becomes solid
3. A solid that has atoms arranged in a repeating pattern
4. Type of rock that has been changed by high temperature and high pressure
5. All the different paths rocks might take as they change from one rock type to another rock type
6. Type of rock that is made of small particles of rock and minerals cemented together

Big Idea Review

1. **List** In your own words, list the properties an object must have in order to be called a mineral.

2. **Recall** Why would we not be able to find any of the original rocks that formed on Earth?

3. **Explain** Why is color not a good property to use to identify minerals?

4. **Sequence** Draw a graphic organizer to show how sediment becomes a sedimentary rock.

5. **Draw Conclusions** Suppose while walking along a mountain trail, you find a fossil of a fish. What conclusions can you make about the land where you found the fossil?

6. **Generalize** What has to happen to metamorphic rock before it can become igneous rock?

Write About The Rock Cycle

Explain What are three different ways a sedimentary rock can change as it moves through the rock cycle?

CHAPTER 3

EARTH SCIENCE EXPERT: LAPIDARY

Do You Like to Make Beautiful Things? A Lapidary Does Just That!

People who work with minerals and gemstones are called lapidaries. Think about pieces of jewelry that contain diamonds, rubies, or other precious stones. These gemstones are rare and beautiful minerals. How do rough and unpolished gems turn into the shiny, beautiful shapes found in jewelry? That is the job of a lapidary. Erik Martinez is a master lapidary.

What does someone in your profession do?

I design cut or carved gemstones. I take raw, rough, or uncut gemstones and use diamond wheels or diamond points to carve them into pieces of art. I supply jewelers with gemstones that they can use to make their own jewelry. Collectors also keep gemstones in their collections.

Erik Martinez designs and cuts gemstones for jewelers and collectors.

When you were younger, did you ever imagine yourself where you are now?

No, not at all. But, when I was about 5 or 6 years old, I would take my father's hammer, put on goggles and go to my backyard and break open rocks. I couldn't wait to see what was inside every rock I came across. I would also bug my father to take me to the local rock shop. One day, the owner gave me a free piece of orbicular poppy jasper, and I was hooked!

This rock is called orbicular poppy jaspar. How many different colors can you see in the rock?

What kinds of interests would someone need to have if they wanted to be a lapidary?

I think someone would need a good sense of nature and of the things it contains, plus a natural interest in Earth objects. They should also have a strong fascination with any type of rock, mineral, and all aspects of geology.

What is your typical workday like?

First, I work in the office, taking care of customers and paperwork. I spend the rest of the day in my cutting and designing studio creating fabulous gemstones.

What advice would you give young people who are interested in gemstones and lapidary work?

Go to the library or bookstore or even shop online for books on minerals, rocks, and gemstones. Then, like me, ask your parents to take you to a gem show so you can see many of the gems and minerals in person. There is nothing like holding that first beautiful gemstone and imagining what you could do with it.

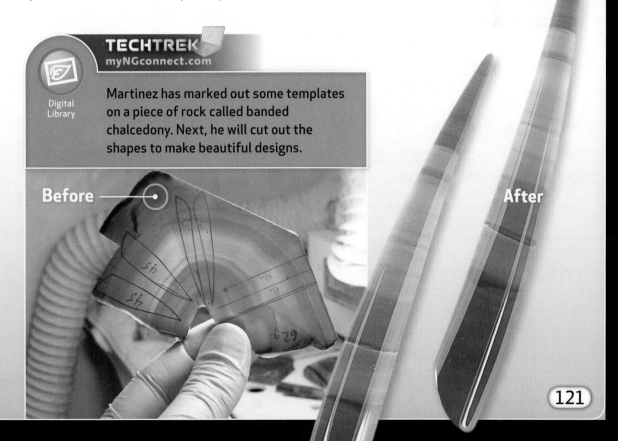

Martinez has marked out some templates on a piece of rock called banded chalcedony. Next, he will cut out the shapes to make beautiful designs.

Before

After

BECOME AN EXPERT

Metals: Hard-Working Minerals

Some of the most useful minerals are metals, such as iron, aluminum, and gold. You'd be surprised how many products you use every day are made from these and other metals. Let's take a closer look at metals.

All metals form in Earth's crust as a result of the **rock cycle** . As rocks form and change, so do some of the minerals that make them up. Some metals found in **sedimentary** rocks are pieces of other types of rock.

TECHTREK
myNGconnect.com

Digital Library

This is how copper looks right from the ground. The shiny copper fills cracks in rock.

rock cycle

The **rock cycle** is a series of actions that changes rocks from one type to another.

sedimentary

Sedimentary rock forms from small pieces of rocks and minerals that are cemented together.

TECHTREK
myNGconnect.com

Student
eEdition

Digital
Library

Some metals form from hot gases and liquids. These gases and liquids rise up through the rock from deep below the surface. As they rise, they deposit metals, such as copper, in the cracks in the rocks.

Copper deposits often cover a large area. The copper is dug from the ground in huge open pits like the one shown below.

Sometimes metals, such as gold, silver and copper, form in a pure state. This means that they can be mined from the ground and used just as they are. Other metals are part of another mineral and must be separated from it. For example, the metal iron makes up part of the mineral hematite. The metal titanium makes up part of the mineral rutile.

Copper is mined in this open-pit mine in Indonesia.

123

Gold Gold forms in **metamorphic** rocks. Gold is a popular metal for jewelry because it has a beautiful color and can be shaped easily. It can be pounded into extremely thin sheets of gold foil. This foil is used to coat statues and parts of buildings for decoration. Shreds of this gold foil are even used as a decoration on desserts! People can eat these small amounts of gold without harm.

Gold has a place in space, too. It's used as a coating on satellites to protect them from the strong rays of the sun. Gold is even part of the helmets worn by astronauts.

Their visors are coated with it. The gold reflects light like a mirror. When astronauts walked on the moon, the gold visor protected their eyes from the sun's harmful rays.

Gold leaf decorates this cake.

Gold foil protected the lower part of the lunar spacecraft from the sun's harmful rays.

metamorphic
Metamorphic rock forms from rock that has been changed by high temperature, high pressure, and hot liquids and gases.

Did you know that gold also is found in cell phones, calculators, and computers? It's used in their circuit boards. In fact, every cell phone has about fifty cents worth of gold in it.

Multiply that by the one billion cell phones made each year. That's a lot of gold! When old cell phones, calculator, and computers are recycled, the gold can be removed and used again.

A gold nugget dug from the ground has the same color and luster as the objects the gold will be used to make.

Gold conducts electricity well. It is used for the circuit boards inside cell phones and other electronics.

Silver Silver also forms in metamorphic rocks. Just as pure gold is made only of **atoms** of gold, pure silver is made only of atoms of silver. Also like gold, silver is shiny and easy to bend and shape. It is used to make musical instruments, jewelry, and coins. Many people have tooth fillings made from silver.

Like gold, silver is used in the circuit boards of cameras and other electronics. The shiny surface of CDs and DVDs also comes from a silver coating.

This is how silver sometimes looks when found in the ground. How could you tell it apart from other rocks in the ground?

These horns are coated with silver.

atoms

An **atom** is the smallest piece of matter that can still be identified as that matter.

Silver's color, luster, and ease of shaping have long made it useful in jewelry.

Scientists have recently discovered that very tiny particles of silver can kill bacteria and viruses. Companies are developing silver products that can help fight the spread of disease. One such product is a drinking glass that has a thin film of silver on its surface. The silver kills 99.9% of all bacteria that come in contact with the surface. This product would be very useful in places such as hospitals, where cleanliness is extremely important. Some bandages are lined with silver to prevent infections. This is especially important in cases where bandages have to be changed often, such as for burn victims.

These socks contain silver. The silver is supposed to kill the bacteria that cause smelly feet.

Comprehensive footcare using nano silver technology

Prevents bacteria and fungus causing itchiness and smells

Sole UK Importer
JR Nanotech Plc
www.jrnanotech.com

BECOME AN EXPERT

Titanium Titanium is a metal that can be mined from a large variety of rocks and minerals. Today, titanium is usually mined from the **igneous** rock anorthosite. Titanium forms in the needlelike **crystals** of the mineral rutile. In its pure form, titanium is easy to bend and shape. It doesn't rust easily.

When titanium is combined with other metals such as zinc, aluminum, or tin, it becomes very strong and difficult to break. Titanium is also much lighter in weight compared to other metals with similar properties.

The properties of strength, light weight, and rust resistance make titanium ideal for use in sporting goods. Golf clubs, bicycles, tennis rackets, and baseball bats are some things made with titanium.

The needlelike crystals of rutile grow inside this clear quartz crystal.

Racers on bicycles made of lightweight titanium have an advantage over riders on heavier bicycles.

igneous
Igneous rock forms when melted rock cools and becomes solid.

crystal
A **crystal** is a solid that has atoms arranged in a repeating pattern.

Because titanium does not react with body fluids, fleshy tissue, or bone, it can be placed inside the human body. Today titanium is used to make artificial hips, joints, jawbones, and other body parts.

Artificial legs and arms are usually strapped to the outside of a person's body. This can cause the skin in that area to become sore and numb. In 2006, doctors in London developed an artificial finger that can be connected directly to a person's skeleton. A titanium rod connects the finger directly to the bone. Even though the titanium rod goes through the skin, infection is not a problem. The skin grows and forms a seal around the metal, keeping germs out. Doctors are hoping someday to connect artificial arms and legs to bone.

Deer antlers pierce the deer's skin without causing infection. Doctors studied deer antlers to learn how titanium rods can be designed to attach artificial limbs to a person's skeleton without causing infection.

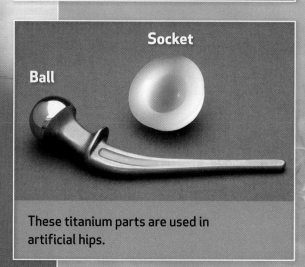

Socket

Ball

These titanium parts are used in artificial hips.

BECOME AN EXPERT

Mercury One of the most unusual metals is mercury. It is the only metal that is liquid at room temperature. Mercury is also called quicksilver because it looks like liquid silver and flows very quickly. Most mercury comes from the mineral cinnabar. If you heat the cinnabar, mercury oozes from it! But you wouldn't want to do that. Mercury is a poison.

Mercury was used in thermometers. But because it is a poison, most thermometers now use red-colored alcohol. Mercury is still useful, though. Street lights and other lights contain mercury gas because it gives off a lot of light when electricity runs through it.

Silver-colored mercury comes from the reddish mineral cinnabar, often found near volcanoes and hot springs.

Mercury gas glows when electricity passes through it. This property makes mercury useful for lighting.

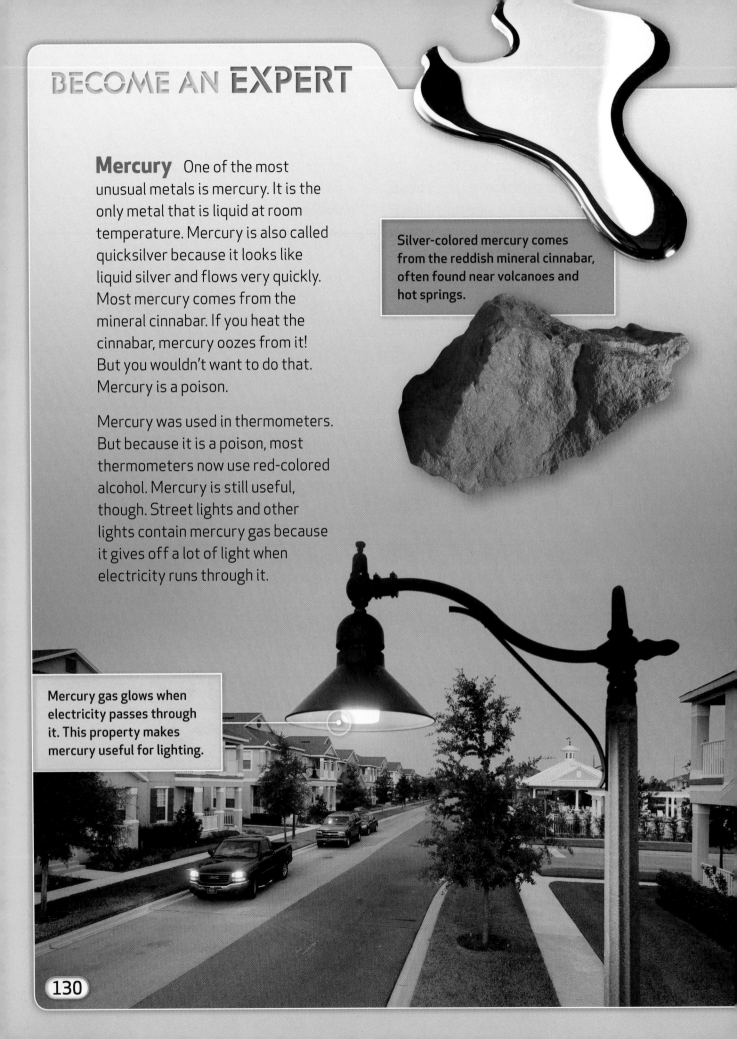

Aluminum Next to iron, aluminum is the most widely used metal. Like any metal, its properties make it useful. Aluminum is easily pressed and shaped into thin sheets. The result is aluminum foil! Aluminum is lightweight yet strong when mixed with other metals. So aluminum is used in almost every kind of vehicle—cars, trucks, ships, planes, trains, and bicycles.

Aluminum conducts, or carries, heat easily. So it's used for pots and pans. This metal reflects light very well, so it's used as a coating on glass to make mirrors. Its shininess also makes it a hit at birthday parties. Those shiny, silvery balloons are coated with aluminum.

Earth's rocks provide a wealth of metals and other minerals. Scientists continue to study their properties to find new uses for these resources.

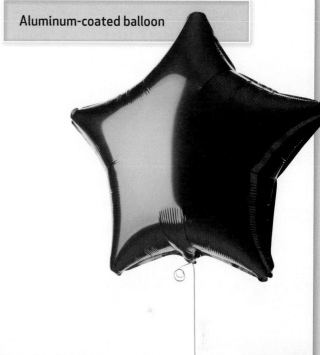

Aluminum-coated balloon

Rolls of aluminum are used to make many products, such as car doors and highway signs.

CHAPTER 3

SHARE AND COMPARE

Turn and Talk Some of the most useful minerals are metals. How are metals useful in everyday life? Form a complete answer to this question together with a partner.

Read Choose two pages in this section. Practice reading the pages. Then read them aloud to a partner. Talk about why the pages are interesting.

my SCIENCE notebook **Write** Write a conclusion that tells the important ideas about useful metals. State what you think is the Big Idea of this section. Share what you wrote with a classmate. Compare your conclusions. Did your classmate make the connection between a metal's properties and its uses?

my SCIENCE notebook **Draw** Work in small groups. Think of a use for one of the metals you read about. Draw a picture showing that use. Using the drawings, create a large poster showing the many uses of metals.

HOW CAN WE PROTECT EARTH'S RESOURCES?

Think about what you did this morning. When you did these things, you used Earth's resources—air, water, plants, fuel, and more. People share these resources with all living things, now and in the future. By taking care of Earth and by using only what you need, you can be sure that everyone has their share.

This picture shows the Brooklyn Bridge and New York City. The red and yellow colors show areas that are giving off a lot of heat. Resources are used to produce this heat.

TECHTREK
myNGconnect.com

134   135

After reading Chapter 4, you will be able to:

- Identify that Earth has both renewable and nonrenewable resources.
  RESOURCES FROM EARTH

- Explain that Earth's resources are important for human activity, but humans can affect or damage Earth's resources. **RENEWABLE RESOURCES, NONRENEWABLE RESOURCES**

- Identify ways Earth's renewable resources can be maintained. **RENEWABLE RESOURCES**

- Identify ways Earth's nonrenewable resources can be maintained.
  NONRENEWABLE RESOURCES

- Identify ways Earth's nonrenewable energy resources can be maintained.
  NONRENEWABLE ENERGY RESOURCES

- Identify Earth's renewable energy sources. **RENEWABLE ENERGY RESOURCES**

- Science in a Snap! Explain that Earth's resources are important for human activity, but humans can affect or damage Earth's resources. **RENEWABLE RESOURCES**

HOW CAN WE PROTECT EARTH RES

Think about what you did this morning. When you did these things, you used Earth's resources—air, water, plants, fuel, and more. People share these resources with all living things, now and in the future. By taking care of Earth and by using only what you need, you can be sure that everyone has their share.

TECHTREK

myNGconnect.com

Student
eEdition

Vocabulary
Games

Digital
Library

Enrichment
Activities

H'S OURCES?

This picture shows the Brooklyn Bridge and New York City. The red and yellow colors show areas that are giving off a lot of heat. Resources are used to produce this heat.

SCIENCE VOCABULARY

renewable resources
(ri-NŪ-ah-bl RĒ-sors-es)

Renewable resources are those that are always being replaced and will not run out. (p. 139)

> Water is a renewable resource. It will not run out.

nonrenewable resources
(non-ri-NŪ-ah-bl RĒ-sors-es)

Nonrenewable resources are those that cannot be replaced quickly enough to keep from running out. (p. 139)

> Earth's supply of oil will run out. It is a nonrenewable resource.

pollution (puh-LŪ-shun)

Pollution is the presence of substances that are harmful to the environment or to living things. (p. 141)

> Smoke from factories is one kind of pollution.

my Science Vocabulary

biomass
(BĪ-ō-mas)

fossil fuel
(FOS-il FYŪ-ehl)

hydroelectric power
(hī-drō-eh-LEK-trik POW-ur)

nonrenewable resources
(non-ri-NŪ-ah-bl RĒ-sors-es)

pollutioan
(puh-LŪ-shun)

renewable resources
(ri-NŪ-ah-bl RĒ-sors-es)

TECHTREK
myNGconnect.com

Vocabulary Games

fossil fuel (FOS-il FYŪ-ehl)

A **fossil fuel** is any fuel that formed from the remains of plants and animals that lived millions of years ago. (p. 158)

Coal is the most plentiful fossil fuel found in the United States.

hydroelectric power (hī-drō-eh-LEK-trik POW-ur)

Hydroelectric power is electricity produced by the energy in moving water. (p. 162)

Hydroelectric power has been used in the United States for over one hundred years.

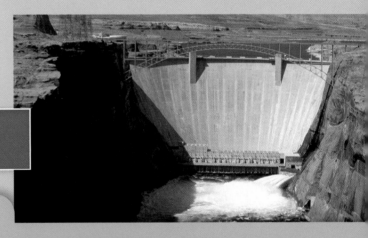

biomass (BĪ-ō-mas)

Biomass is plant material and animal waste used as fuel. (p. 163)

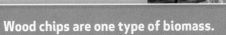

Wood chips are one type of biomass.

Resources from Earth

Observe the Grand Canyon Skywalk pictured on these pages. The Skywalk has a glass floor to allow a breathtaking view of the canyon. It has a metal frame made of steel that moves slightly when the wind or temperature changes. Where do you think the building materials in the Skywalk came from? Both steel and glass are made from resources found in the ground.

Everything you use comes from Earth's resources. It takes resources to build walkways, bridges, and tall buildings. But even little things—a toothpick or a penny—are made from resources.

Air is a natural resource.

Cotton cloth is made from natural resources.

Metal is made from natural resources.

Water is a natural resource.

Some resources are **nonrenewable resources**. These resources cannot be replaced quickly enough to keep from running out. Coal is nonrenewable. It forms over millions of years from buried plant remains. People use coal faster than it can be replaced. Eventually Earth will run out of coal.

Other resources are **renewable resources**. They are always being replaced and will not run out if used responsibly. Trees are renewable. When seeds drop from trees, new trees grow. Or, trees can be replaced by replanting.

Glass is made from natural resources.

Rock is a natural resource.

TECHTREK
myNGconnect.com

Digital Library

Visitors to the Grand Canyon Skywalk in Arizona must wear shoe covers to protect the clear glass floor. What resources are found or used in this photo?

Before You Move On

1. What are renewable resources?
2. How are trees renewed?
3. **Apply** Does a sun-powered calculator run on a renewable resource? Use what you know about renewable resources to explain your answer.

Renewable Resources

Lakes, forests, caves, and rivers are some of the natural features in Missouri that attract visitors. Observe the photo of a lake. What resources do you observe? Which ones are renewable? Water, wildlife, air, and trees are all renewable.

These resources are important, but not just for visitors. They are an important part of everyone's life, every day. You depend on these resources for water to drink, food to eat, and air to breathe.

Some resources depend on other resources to survive. Without water or air, plants wouldn't be able to grow. Without plants to eat or water to drink, wildlife wouldn't survive.

Canada geese swim on a lake in St. Louis, Missouri.

AIR
People can help keep air clean by driving cars that use less gasoline.

TREES
People need to replace trees that are cut down. Trees provide homes for animals and restore oxygen to the air.

Plants give off oxygen. Earth's air depends on plants for its level of oxygen. How would you be affected if there were no longer trees putting oxygen into the air?

Pollution can damage Earth's renewable resources. Pollution contains substances that are harmful to the environment. Most pollution is caused by people. Cars and factories are a big source of air pollution. Fertilizers and waste from farm animals can pollute lakes and rivers.

As people depend on resources to live, it is important to take care of them. There are many people on Earth, but only a limited supply of resources.

WATER
You can care for lakes and rivers by not dumping chemicals and garbage into them.

WILDLIFE
To keep wildlife healthy, people must protect animal habitats.

Rivers and streams wind across the land. Lakes dot the landscape. Throughout history, water has been an important resource for human activity. Early explorers and traders traveled on waterways. People settled near rivers and lakes. For food, people depended on fish and animals that lived in or near the water.

Water resources are just as important today. Do you like to fish, kayak, water ski, or swim? Rivers and lakes provide opportunities for many types of fun. People build homes along shorelines to enjoy the view and the water activities.

These people enjoy sailing on the Charles River, near Boston.

The Connecticut River provides opportunities for boating, fishing, and other kinds of fun.

Factories are often built next to rivers or lakes to make use of the nearby water. The water is used to wash away waste and to dissolve chemicals. Waterways are used to ship supplies to the factory. Later, they are used to ship finished products out of the factory.

Farmers use water from rivers and lakes for their crops. Farm crops are also moved by boat or barge along waterways to markets to be sold. As you can see, people depend on water resources for many things.

Barges on a river near Portland, Oregon, transport goods to and from factories.

The Colorado River provides water for these lettuce plants in California.

The drinking water for a city often comes from a river or lake. Water for farm crops and gardens may come from the same source. If too much water is used, a water shortage develops.

People sometimes build dams to hold back the water in a river to form a lake.

Water from the lake can be used for crops or for a town's water supply. Dams can have some negative side effects. The lake formed by a dam covers land once used by people and land animals. Some fish and water animals also cannot survive in their changed environment.

A drought, or long period with no rain, caused this lake to dry up. The place where boats entered the lake has been closed.

Ships travel down the Calumet river in Chicago, Illinois, to industries such as steel mills, oil refineries, and chemical plants.

Shasta Dam, on the Sacramento River in California, is used to produce electricity.

The activities of people can sometimes affect the quality of water. Chemicals like weed killers, oil, and paint may wash into rivers and cause water pollution. Water can also be polluted by human and animal waste.

Pollution can also change the rain. Many cars and smokestacks spew smoke into the air. The smoke can be full of chemicals. The chemicals can mix with water droplets in clouds. This forms a weak acid. The rain that falls from the clouds is called acid rain. Acid rain affects many of Earth's renewable resources, such as plants, water, and animals.

Science in a Snap! Acid Rain

Vinegar is a weak acid. Limestone contains calcium. Some buildings and statues contain calcium, too.

Drop a piece of limestone into a cup of vinegar. Leave it in the cup for 24 hours.

What happened to the limestone? How is your experiment like the effect of acid rain on buildings?

What can you do to make sure there is enough clean water to go around? You can start by not wasting water.

- Turn off the faucet when you brush your teeth.
- Don't run the washing machine or dishwasher when it is not full.
- Water the grass or garden only when necessary.
- Spread mulch around trees and plants to hold moisture.
- Avoid long showers.

Sewage is the wastewater from homes and businesses that goes into underground pipes. It travels to a sewage treatment plant, where it is cleaned. The clean water flows back into waterways. Chemicals such as paint or motor oil are hard to clean from water. They should not be poured down the drain. In most towns or communities, they can be taken to special collection sites.

TECHTREK
myNGconnect.com

These people are saving water by using a bucket and sponge. They spray the car only when they're ready to rinse it.

Enrichment Activities

When it rains, water runs into drains along the street. But this water does not go to a sewage treatment plant. It goes straight into our waterways. It carries litter that was dumped in the gutter, weed killers washed from yards, and animal droppings. You can help keep waterways clean by using products that won't harm the Earth and by picking up after your pets.

The storm drain in this picture is near the ocean. The sign explains where rainwater and anything else that washes down this drain will go.

Lake Mead supplies water to large cities such as Las Vegas and Los Angeles. It also supplies water to farms.

old water level

Before You Move On

1. Where does rainwater go after it runs into street drains, and what does it carry with it?
2. Explain how factories make use of water resources.
3. **Draw Conclusions** Water is renewable and will not run out, so why is it important to protect it?

Nonrenewable Resources

Do your clothes have plastic or metal snaps or zippers? If your answer is yes, then you are wearing nonrenewable resources. Metals and plastics are made from resources that take millions of years to form. People use nonrenewable resources faster than they are replaced.

Buildings use large amounts of nonrenewable resources. Observe the construction site in the photo. What are some of the nonrenewable resources that are being used?

Steel is a strong metal. It is made mostly from iron. Builders use steel to make a building's frame. Concrete is a mix of different resources, including limestone, sand, rocks, and water. Builders use concrete for many things, such as floors and columns. Glass is made mainly from melted sand. Sand is another nonrenewable resource. Almost all buildings have glass windows.

glass

MATERIAL	MAIN INGREDIENTS (NONRENEWABLE RESOURCES)	USES
STEEL	iron ore	beams construction cranes
GLASS	melted sand	windows
CONCRETE	sand, gravel, or crushed rocks	floors, columns

The construction of this building uses materials that come from nonrenewable resources.

concrete

steel

Look around you—metals are almost everywhere. Metals form deep underground. Many of the metals you are most familiar with are taken from certain rocks, called ores. Aluminum, copper, tin, and silver are some of the metals found in ores. Other metals such as steel and bronze are made by combining metals with different substances.

Iron and steel are used in construction and for making car parts. Food cans are made of steel. Used iron and steel can be recycled.

Aluminum is the most commonly occurring metal in Earth's surface. You see aluminum every time you drink from a can.

RECYCLING **STEEL**

Workers are breaking down this steel ship for recycling.

The steel scraps are melted in a furnace.

Aluminum can be recycled again and again. It can be used to make new cans, car parts, or other products.

Copper is a reddish-brown metal. You have probably seen copper pipes or copper electric wires. Copper can be recycled to make new products.

Metal ores are a nonrenewable resource. Earth's supply is limited. By recycling metals, you can help prevent Earth's supply from running out. Recycling saves energy, too. Making new metal uses more energy than recycling metal does. You can save energy by using recycled metal instead of new metal.

Melted steel is made into standard shapes.

The standard shapes are made into steel beams or other finished products.

Earth's nonrenewable resources will last longer if people practice the three Rs—reduce, reuse, and recycle.

Glass is made from sand. The sand is melted at a very high temperature until it becomes syrupy. Then it is shaped and cooled. Billions of glass containers are made each year. Most of these containers can be washed and reused again and again.

Glass that is no longer needed can be recycled.

Buying recycled glass instead of new glass is better for the environment. Why? The process of mining sand and making new glass takes a lot of energy. It can cause air and water pollution. Making a bottle from recycled glass takes half as much energy as making it from new glass.

This pile of sand will be used to make glass in this bottle-making factory.

REDUCE

Be careful not to waste nonrenewable resources. You should use only what you need.

REUSE

You can reuse many nonrenewable resources. When a stone building is torn down, the stone is still useful. It can be reused to make fireplaces or garden paths and walls.

This worker checks new glass bottles made from recycled glass.

This worker is emptying glass bottles at a recycling center. The bottles will be melted down to make new bottles.

RECYCLE

You can recycle metal and glass. This saves nonrenewable resources.

Observe the products pictured here. Would you guess they are made from a black liquid that was pumped out of the ground? These and thousands of other products are made from oil. Most plastics, from cell phones to garbage bags, are made from oil. So are nylon and polyester items— fleece jackets, backpacks, tents, and nylon rope. Oil is even used in hand lotions and house paint.

Oil is nonrenewable. It will someday run out. But there are ways to make it last longer. Remember the three Rs? You can reduce, reuse, and recycle to extend the supply of oil.

Oil is used in products like this hand soap.

Plastic for this bottle came from oil.

Plastic for these pens was made from oil.

Try to *reduce* the number of plastic products you buy. Do you really need water in a disposable plastic bottle? If not, do not buy it.

Think of ways to *reuse* the plastic products you already have. Use old plastic shopping bags to carry trash. Give the nylon or polyester jacket you outgrew to someone who needs it.

Finally, be sure to *recycle* what you can. Have you noticed a triangular recycling symbol on plastic products? Inside the symbol is a number, or code, that tells the type of plastic. Check with your recycling center to see which plastics they can use.

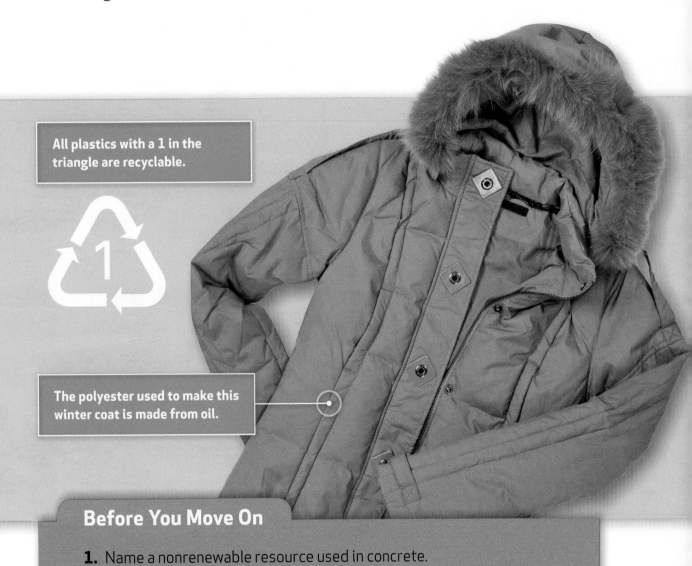

All plastics with a 1 in the triangle are recyclable.

The polyester used to make this winter coat is made from oil.

Before You Move On

1. Name a nonrenewable resource used in concrete.
2. In what ways are iron and steel alike?
3. **Predict** In the future, do you think we will still have cell phones, hand lotion, and other products that are currently made from oil? Explain.

Nonrenewable Energy Resources

What can you observe in this photo? Point to all the uses of energy you can see.

This airport depends on energy to do all kinds of things. Without energy from electricity, airplanes would not have runway lights to guide them to the ground. Inside the airport building would be dark, too.

Airplanes use energy to fly. Their engines burn fuel to make them work. Trucks on the runway couldn't drive supplies and luggage back and forth from the airplane and the airport without energy. In fact, all cars, trucks, and buses depend on energy to get from one place to another.

This airport in Texas uses different forms of energy to function.

Large airports have thousands of computers. Workers and passengers rely on computers to find their airplanes. Each computer uses about as much energy as a couple of light bulbs.

Travelers walk through airports that are heated or cooled with energy. They may stop to buy a snack. Food is heated or cooled using energy.

When you look around at an airport, or even at school or on the street, people are using energy everywhere. Where do think all of this energy comes from? In the United States today, most of it comes from burning nonrenewable resources.

Fossil fuels provide much of the world's energy. A fossil fuel is any fuel that formed from the remains of plants and animals that lived millions of years ago. All fossil fuels are found underground. People have to dig mines or drill into the ground to get them out. Coal, oil, and natural gas are all fossil fuels. They are nonrenewable resources.

Coal, oil, and natural gas don't look like plants or animals. Use the diagram below to see how they changed. The remains first had to be buried under layer after layer of mud and rock. The weight of the layers above created pressure and heat. Gradually, this pressure and heat caused the remains to transform into fossil fuels.

Oil and natural gas formed from dead plants and animals that sank to the ocean floor 300–400 million years ago.

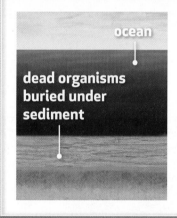

ocean

dead organisms buried under sediment

oil forming

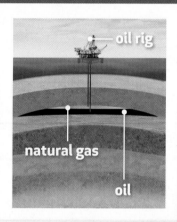

oil rig

natural gas

oil

Oil rigs are built to remove oil and natural gas that's under the ocean floor.

Fossil fuels contain energy. Would you believe this energy came from the sun? Plants took in the sun's energy and stored it. When animals ate the plants, the energy was passed on to them. The sun's energy was stored in their remains over millions of years. Today when people burn coal, oil, or natural gas, the stored energy is released as heat energy.

People use fossil fuels for many energy needs. Natural gas is used to heat water and warm homes. Oil-based fuels are used in cars, trucks, and aircraft. Coal is used in power plants to help make electricity. As Earth's population increases, the demand for fossil fuels increases, too. Eventually, Earth will run out of fossil fuels.

Trains transport coal to power plants, where the coal is burned to produce electricity.

Before You Move On

1. List three fossil fuels.
2. Explain how fossil fuels form.
3. **Evaluate** A poster shows a gas pump. It says, "Energy From the Sun." Does the poster make sense? Explain.

Renewable Energy Resources

Renewable resources, such as sunlight and wind, can be used as energy sources. Unlike fossil fuels, these resources will not run out.

Do you have a solar calculator? It contains a tiny solar cell. The solar cell uses sunlight to make electricity. What if you wanted to power a whole house, or even a city? For more power, solar panels are used. The panels contain thousands of solar cells.

Sometimes solar power plants use curved mirrors to direct or focus sunlight. The energy from sunlight causes the water to heat up and make steam. The steam turns the blades of a turbine. The turbine runs a generator that produces electricity.

TECHTREK
myNGconnect.com

Digital Library

This worker is carrying a solar panel.

In windy locations, the energy in wind can be used to make electricity. Wind farms, such as the one pictured here, contain many wind turbines grouped together. A wind turbine has wing-like blades. Where the blades meet, there is a generator. The wind spins the blades of the turbine. This runs the generator, the machine that makes the electricity. Most wind turbines are tall to catch the strong, steady winds high above the ground. Some turbines can turn or tilt when the wind changes direction.

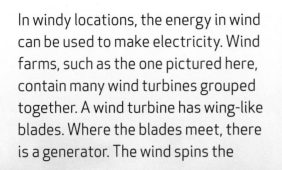 This wind farm is located off the coast of Denmark. Winds are usually stronger at sea.

Even on a still day, rafts and inner tubes can float down a river. The raft moves along with the water. Moving water is a renewable source of energy.

Electricity produced by the energy in moving water is called **hydroelectric power**. Dams are built on rivers to produce hydroelectric power. The dam holds back some of the water in the river. This forms a lake or reservoir. A controlled amount of water is allowed to flow from the reservoir. The flowing water spins the blades of a turbine, and the turbine runs a generator that makes electricity.

The Glen Canyon Dam in Arizona uses water from the Colorado River to generate hydroelectric power.

Biomass is plant material and animal waste used as fuel. It is a renewable source of energy. Biomass materials have energy stored from plants and animals. Your trash has some types of biomass that can be reused. Any paper products that you couldn't recycle count as plant material. So do banana peels and other food products. Your trash also may have animal waste, or things that came from animals, such as eggshells.

Biomass can be used to make electricity. The biomass is burned to heat water and make steam. The steam is used to make electricity.

Sometimes biomass is used to make fuels for cars and trucks. Ethanol is a fuel made from corn or other crops. Biodiesel fuel is made from plant or animal oils—even oil left over from making French fries!

This industrial waste plant burns trash and other waste to generate electricity.

The burning of fossil fuels for energy causes air pollution. It releases carbon dioxide into the air, which contributes to acid rain. Acid rain is a problem for plants and animals, as well as some buildings. Extra carbon dioxide in the air is also causing Earth to get warmer. A warming global climate is quickly changing the habitats of living things everywhere.

As you can see, burning fossil fuels harms the environment. One day, Earth's supply will run out. Yet fossil fuels are the most widely used source of energy in the United States.

Scientists today are working on developing energy sources that do not harm the environment.

What are the energy resources of the future? This is a big question. Some possible answers are sunlight, wind, moving water, and biomass. These are all renewable resources, and cleaner than fossil fuels. Still, no option is perfect. The chart on the next page gives you some of the pros and cons of each one.

These solar panels are used to collect light energy from the sun.

SOME **ENERGY RESOURCES**

	PROS	CONS
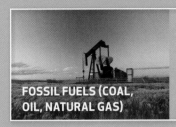 **FOSSIL FUELS (COAL, OIL, NATURAL GAS)**	• Affordable and available	• Nonrenewable: will run out • Cause pollution, harm the environment • Prices are rising
 **SOLAR**	• Renewable: won't run out • No pollution	• Less sun on cloudy days, none at night • Takes up a lot of space • Panels are costly
 **WIND**	• Renewable: won't run out • No pollution	• Wind not always blowing • Takes a lot of space, can be noisy • May harm birds
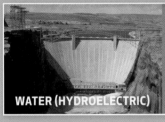 **WATER (HYDROELECTRIC)**	• Renewable: won't run out • Low pollution	• Dams are costly • Can destroy the habitats of living things
 **BIOMASS**	• Renewable: won't run out • Low pollution • Can use garbage	• Farmland used for fuel crops rather than food crops

Before You Move On

1. What does a solar cell do?
2. Use the chart on this page. What are some disadvantages of installing solar panels?
3. **Draw Conclusions** Why do you think we continue to use fossil fuels for energy even when we know they harm the environment?

SAVING RESOURCES

This is not an ordinary picture of a house! Most cameras capture visible light. But the camera that took this photograph captures heat. Usually, you can only feel heat. With this camera though, you can see it. The parts that are colored white are the hottest. The parts that are red and yellow are a little cooler, but they are still warm. The parts that are blue are the coolest. The warmest areas are where the most heat is escaping.

In places where winters are cool, people use a lot of energy to keep their homes and other buildings warm. When heat escapes, energy is wasted. Use the photo to see where heat is escaping from this house. Observe the windows. They are a cool blue. That's because the owners replaced them. The new windows have two layers to seal in heat. Observe the rest of the house. Where does the most heat escape? If you lived in this house, what could you do to use less energy?

You can do some things at home to prevent heat and energy loss. Sealing cracks in window frames or walls helps keep warm air in and cool air out. Cool air that seeps inside has to be heated, wasting more energy. Sometimes, there is nothing between the outside wall of a home and the inside. Just like having more than one layer of glass in a window, having more than one layer for the roof or walls helps seal in heat.

Did you know that devices that are plugged in use energy even when they are not in use. Just like vampires, plugs continually drain energy and pass it along as heat. Look at the picture below. The red color shows that heat is been lost. How do you stop these vampires? Just unplug them.

When a home is well sealed and cared for, energy is saved. Saving energy saves natural resources.

These plugs are still using electricity even though the devices they are connected to are turned off.

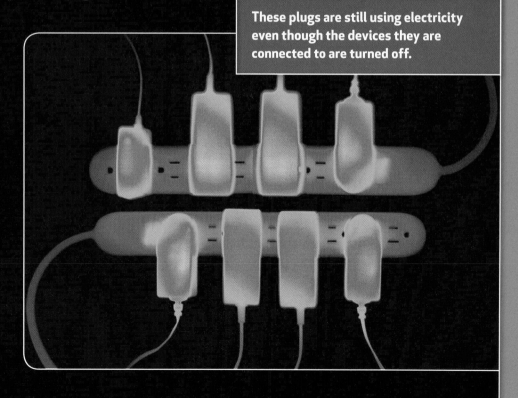

167

Conclusion

Some of Earth's resources are renewable and won't run out, if they are used wisely. For example, water is renewable, but it can be polluted or overused. Rocks, metals, and fossil fuels are nonrenewable resources. These resources will run out. You can help make them last longer by using the three Rs—reduce, reuse, and recycle. Fossil fuels supply most of the energy, such as electricity, that people use. Other sources include wind, sun, water, and biomass. Each source has pros and cons.

Big Idea People can protect Earth's resources by using renewable resources wisely and by reducing, reusing, and recycling nonrenewable resources.

Reduce

Be careful not to waste nonrenewable resources. You should use only what you need.

Reuse

You can reuse many nonrenewable resources. When a stone building is torn down, the stone is still useful. It can be reused to make fireplaces or garden paths and walls.

Recycle

You can recycle metal and glass. This saves nonrenewable resources.

Vocabulary Review

Match the following terms with the correct definition.

A. hydroelectric power

B. fossil fuel

C. nonrenewable resources

D. biomass

E. renewable resources

F. pollution

1. Plant material and animal waste used as fuel
2. Electricity produced by the energy in moving water
3. Resources that are always being replaced and will not run out
4. Any fuel that formed from the remains of plants and animals that lived millions of years ago
5. Resources that cannot be replaced quickly enough to keep from running out
6. The presence of substances that are harmful to the environment or to living things

Big Idea Review

1. **Recall** What do you call electricity produced by moving water?

2. **List** Make a list of two renewable resources and two nonrenewable resources you have used today.

3. **Explain** How does acid rain form?

4. **Classify** Make a two-column chart. In the chart, classify the following resources as renewable or nonrenewable: wind, biomass, oil, natural gas, moving water, coal, and sunlight.

5. **Generalize** What do you think are the two biggest cons to the use of fossil fuels for energy?

6. **Predict** You know that aluminum can be recycled again and again. Do you think recycling can make our supply of aluminum last forever? Explain.

Write About Vampire Electricity

Apply What could your school do to reduce vampire power? Write a statement to your school principal describing one step he or she could take to reduce vampire power and save energy.

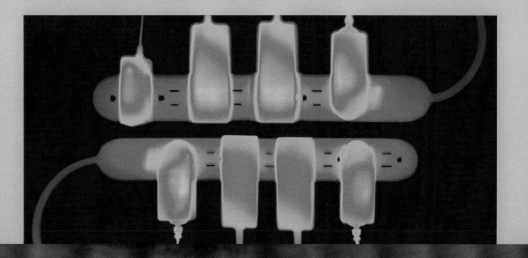

CHAPTER 4 — EARTH SCIENCE EXPERT: ENERGY RESEARCHER

How will energy be produced in the future? Ask an energy researcher.

Want to study about energy sources? Energy researcher Rebecca Dodder talks about her work.

What is your job like?

I work on a team of scientists with the U.S. Environmental Protection Agency (EPA). My role on the team is to study how we might use biomass instead of fossil fuels. I look at ways we can use things like corn, trees, grasses, and algae as energy resources.

What is the connection between your work and Earth science?

My research looks at how we can use biomass to make energy responsibly. At the same time, we need to protect Earth's resources. Wherever people grow and harvest biomass, it affects the whole ecosystem—the soil, water, air, and other plants and animals. If we decide to grow a lot of biomass for energy and fuels, we need to understand how that affects Earth.

Dodder uses computer software that works somewhat like a computer game to model what the future may look like.

TECHTREK
myNGconnect.com

Student
eEdition

Digital
Library

What is the coolest part of your job?

The coolest part of my job is the chance to think creatively and study new technologies. For example, could we really use plants to make fuels to replace gasoline in our vehicles?

What advice do you have for someone who wants to do what you do?

Always ask questions, try to do things that are difficult, and don't be afraid to fail. This is all part of learning, and when you are a scientist, you are constantly learning. Work on your math skills and get a strong education in science. But follow other interests, too.

What do you hope to accomplish?

I've always wanted to make life better for people. One way to do that is to protect the environment in which we live, breathe, work, and play. I want my work to help others make good choices about energy.

TECHTREK
myNGconnect.com

Digital
Library

Dodder researches questions such as "How does growing corn for biomass affect the environment?"

BECOME AN EXPERT

It's Easy Being Green

People everywhere are talking about being "green." But they're not discussing colors. They're talking about saving energy and taking care of the environment.

Do you want to be green? Most people want to keep from harming the environment. But sometimes being green doesn't sound like much fun. Few people want to get rid of their computers, freeze all winter, or quit buying their favorite stuff. Good news—you don't have to! It's really pretty easy being green.

Going by bike instead of by car uses less fossil fuels.

TECHTREK
myNGconnect.com

Student
eEdition

Digital
Library

What's the Problem?

There's no doubt that people do have a problem. On average, each person in the United States throws out more than two kilograms (almost five pounds) of trash every day! It sits in landfills until it decays.

Then there's the problem of natural resources. People don't always take good care of Earth's **renewable resources**. And people are using up Earth's limited supply of **nonrenewable resources**. All over the world, people use nonrenewable **fossil fuels** to run cars, heat homes, and make electricity.

TECHTREK
myNGconnect.com

Digital
Library

The trash in this landfill could take millions of years to decompose.

renewable resources

Renewable resources are those that are always being replaced and will not run out.

nonrenewable resources

Nonrenewable resources are those that cannot be replaced quickly enough to keep from running out.

fossil fuel

A fossil fuel is any fuel that formed from the remains of plants and animals that lived millions of years ago.

173

Step One: Trash Clearly there is work to be done, but the work is not hard if you take one step at a time. Let's start with trash. In some cities, trash is burned as **biomass** to make electricity. But in most places, it's up to you to keep trash out of landfills.

Have you noticed all the trash you toss when you unwrap something new?

Try to buy things with less packaging. A whopping one third of all trash is packaging!

Now take a look at the rest of your trash. What things can be recycled? Put things such as glass, paper, and aluminum drink cans in a recycling bin, not in the trash. Congratulations! You are greener already.

Most paper and plastics can be recycled instead of putting them in trash.

biomass
Biomass is plant material and animal waste used as fuel.

Step Two: Fuel If something switches on and off, it probably uses fuel. Cars use fuel, but buildings use even more. It takes fuel to heat, cool, and light them. A lot of that fuel comes from burning coal, which causes air **pollution** . Try these easy fuel-saving ideas.

- Switch to low-energy light bulbs, and turn off lights that aren't being used. When you finish using the computer, unplug it. Otherwise it uses small amounts of power called "vampire power" to remain in standby mode.

- An extra warm room feels good on a cold day. But so does a cozy sweatshirt. Try that instead. On a hot day, use a fan, not an air conditioner.

- If it's safe, walk or bike to school or other places. You'll be healthier and so will the air as you will be saving fossil fuels that cars need to run.

These brothers are walking to school.

pollution
Pollution is the presence of substances that are harmful to the environment or to living things.

Step Three: Water In the United States, one person uses about 380 liters (100 gallons) of water each day. And that's nothing compared to the water used for crops, factories, and **hydroelectric power** . Fortunately, there are many ways to save water.

Do you let the water run while you are scrubbing your dog or washing dishes? It's easy to save water by turning it off when you aren't using it. For drinking, use tap water. If you drink bottled water, you use a lot of extra water. Water is used in the process of making the bottles, cooling the machines, and cleaning the factory. Finally, keep your showers short. Just twenty-five seconds in the shower uses four liters (over one gallon) of water.

Bottled water is no healthier than tap water, and many resources are used to bottle and transport it.

hydroelectric power
Hydroelectric power is electricity produced by the energy in moving water.

Step Four: Excess Stuff

"Is this your mess?" "Clean your room." "Pick this up." Have you heard any of these recently? If so, you may have too much stuff. All your belongings are made from resources, so having more than you need is a waste of resources. Gather up the things you no longer use. Give them away or have a yard sale.

From now on, avoid collecting so much stuff. This doesn't mean you have to do without. Use the library instead of buying new books. Rent DVDs. Pack your lunch in washable containers instead of disposable ones. Write on both sides of your paper. If you need to buy something new, that's fine. But think about it first. By tomorrow, you may change your mind.

This boy is saving resources by buying used toys instead of new ones.

Track Your Progress It's easy being green, but it can be overwhelming at first. Here's a plan for getting started.

BEING GREEN

- Flip back to the page about trash, and try one of the ideas or think of your own. Then use a calendar or a notebook to record what you did.

- Tomorrow try an idea from the page about fuel. Record what you did.

- Continue with the page about water and the page about excess stuff.

- Encourage your family and friends to join you in your efforts!

After a few days, you will have a record of all the things you have done to make Earth a greener place. Best of all, being green will have become a habit—a good habit for you and for Earth!

People in the United States create a lot of trash and use a lot of resources. But more and more Americans are becoming concerned about the environment. They are interested in "being green."

There are other benefits to riding a bike. This bicyclist in New Zealand can go places a car could never take him.

It's easy to make simple changes to reduce trash and waste less energy. For example, you could use the leftover heat in your oven to warm your home. Just open the oven door once it is turned off. Or, you could shut off the tap water while you brush your teeth. Come up with your own ideas! There are more ways to being green than you might think. Simple changes can become habits that will make Earth greener and healthier.

Remember, to protect Earth's resources, people must use them wisely and not pollute them. You can make Earth's supply of nonrenewable resources last longer by reducing, reusing, and recycling.

Compact fluorescent light bulbs use less energy than other light bulbs.

CHAPTER 4

SHARE AND COMPARE

Turn and Talk What does being green mean to you? Form a complete answer to this question together with a partner.

Read Select two pages in this section. Practice reading the pages. Then read them aloud to a partner. Talk about why the pages are interesting.

my SCIENCE notebook

Write Write a conclusion that tells the big ideas about what you have learned about going green. State what you think is the Big Idea of this section. Share what you wrote with a classmate. Compare your conclusions. What changes would you make first to go green?

my SCIENCE notebook

Draw Form groups of four. Create a "How to be Green" booklet. Have each person choose one step. Draw yourself doing something green related to that step. Label your drawing with the name and number of the step, and the type of activity. Then combine the drawings in order from Step 1 to Step 4.

CHAPTER 5

HOW ARE WEATHER AND THE WATER CYCLE CONNECTED?

What do you see in this photo? At first glance, it looks like a storm over the water. But what you're really seeing is a recycling system millions of years old. Earth's surface holds a limited supply of water. Why isn't it used up? The water you use eventually goes back into lakes, rivers, and the ocean. It then rises into the air. It forms clouds. Then it falls to Earth again in rainstorms like this.

TECHTREK
myNGconnect.com

Student eEdition | Vocabulary Games | Digital Library | Enrichment Activities

Water from the ocean rises and forms clouds. You can observe the rain pouring from this storm cloud above the Caribbean Sea.

182   183

After reading Chapter 5, you will be able to:

- Recognize that the atmosphere is a layer of gases, water, and tiny particles that wraps around Earth. **THE AIR AROUND US**

- Identify the effect temperature, air pressure, and humidity have on weather patterns. **WEATHER**

- Identify the water cycle and its importance to Earth. **THE WATER CYCLE**

- Identify weather factors and their effects on the weather. **OBSERVING WEATHER PATTERNS**

- Identify the elements that affect a region's weather and climate patterns. **CLIMATE**

- **Science in a Snap!** Identify the water cycle and its importance to Earth. **THE WATER CYCLE**

HOW ARE WEATHER WATER

What do you see in this photo? At first glance, it looks like a storm over the water. But what you're really seeing is a recycling system millions of years old. Earth's surface holds a limited supply of water. Why isn't it used up? The water you use eventually goes back into lakes, rivers, and the ocean. It then rises into the air. It forms clouds. Then it falls to Earth again in rainstorms like this.

AND THE CYCLE CONNECTED?

Water from the ocean rises and forms clouds. You can observe the rain pouring from this storm cloud above the Caribbean Sea.

SCIENCE VOCABULARY

weather (WE-thur)

Weather is the state of the atmosphere at a certain place and time. (p. 188)

The weather is clear and sunny.

humidity (hyū-MID-it-ē)

Humidity is the amount of water vapor in the air. (p. 189)

Humidity is a main factor that determines weather.

water cycle (WAH-tur SĪ-cul)

The **water cycle** is the constant movement of Earth's water from the surface to the atmosphere and back again. (p. 192)

In the water cycle, Earth's limited supply of water is recycled.

my Science Vocabulary

climate
(CLĪ-mit)

evaporation
(ē-va-por-Ā-shun)

front
(FRUNT)

humidity
(hyū-MID-it-ē)

water cycle
(WAH-tur SĪ-cul)

weather
(WE-thur)

TECHTREK
myNGconnect.com

Vocabulary
Games

evaporation
(ē-va-por-Ā-shun)

Evaporation is a change from the liquid to the gaseous state. (p. 193)

The sun causes evaporation from the water on Earth's surface.

front (FRUNT)

A **front** is the boundary where two different air masses meet. (p. 204)

Different types of fronts bring different types of weather.

direction of front

warm air mass

cold air mass

climate (CLĪ-mit)

Climate is the pattern of weather over a long period of time. (p. 206)

The climate of an area determines the plants and animals that live there.

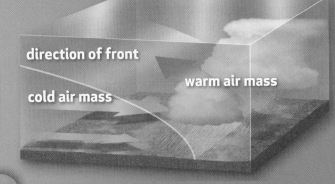

The Air Around Us

The atmosphere is a layer of gases that wraps around Earth like a huge blanket. It holds in Earth's heat, making the planet warm enough for life. The atmosphere contains the air you breathe. It protects living things from the sun's harmful radiation. Earth's atmosphere also helps the planet recycle its water supply.

The atmosphere is made mostly of the gases nitrogen and oxygen. Earth is the only planet in the solar system with an atmosphere formed mostly of these two gases.

Earth's atmosphere also contains countless tiny particles that float in the air. They include soil, pollen grains, and soot from fires. These particles are important for the formation of clouds.

Earth's atmosphere is about 600 km (373 miles) thick. These skydivers are falling through the lowest part of it.

Two other gases play important roles in the atmosphere, although they exist in small amounts. They are carbon dioxide and water vapor.

Carbon dioxide makes up only a fraction of one percent of the atmosphere. But it is a greenhouse gas. That means it is one of the gases that absorbs Earth's heat to keep the planet warm.

Water vapor is a green house gas, too. Water vapor is important because it plays a major role in weather. Without it, there would be no clouds. Without clouds, there would be no precipitation. Earth would be dry and lifeless.

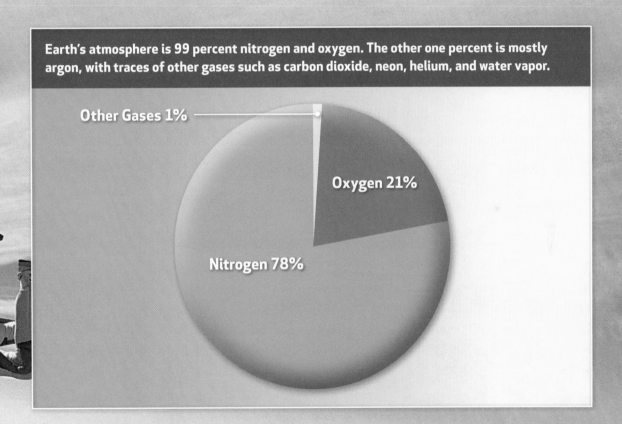

Earth's atmosphere is 99 percent nitrogen and oxygen. The other one percent is mostly argon, with traces of other gases such as carbon dioxide, neon, helium, and water vapor.

Other Gases 1%

Oxygen 21%

Nitrogen 78%

Before You Move On

1. What is the atmosphere?
2. What gas makes up most of Earth's atmosphere?
3. **Evaluate** What are some ways the atmosphere makes life on Earth possible?

Weather

When you get up in the morning, you probably check the day's **weather**. Weather is the state of the atmosphere at a certain place and time. Weather changes from season to season. It changes from day to day. Weather can even change from hour to hour. The sky might be bright and sunny in the morning but turn rainy by afternoon.

We can observe and describe weather by measuring properties of the air. These properties are temperature, humidity, air pressure, and wind. We can also use measurements of these properties to predict weather in the future.

Temperature Look at the photo on this page. Based on what you see, what can you infer about the temperature? There is a lot of snow on the ground and on the trees. The man in this picture is dressed in heavy clothing. The weather must be cold. Temperature is how hot or cold something is.

> Clouds must be at a temperature colder than 0°C (32°F) for snowflakes to form.

Humidity On hot and sticky summer days, the air feels humid. Humidity is the amount of water vapor air can hold. Air that is humid holds a lot of water vapor. It's no surprise that air often feels wetter in summer. Warm air holds more water vapor than cool air. Humidity affects the weather.

Humid air is more likely to produce clouds and precipitation than drier air. Dry air is more likely to come with fair weather.

Observe the weather in the photo below. Do you think the humidity is low or high? The rain is a clue that a lot of moisture is in the air. The weather on this day is hot and humid, so the humidity is high.

The girl in this photo is on Lombok Island, in Indonesia. Lombok Island has warm and humid weather all year long.

Air Pressure Imagine the water pressure you feel at the bottom of a swimming pool. Earth's atmosphere is similar. Like water, air has weight. You live at the bottom of Earth's atmosphere, so there is a lot of air above you. The force of the weight of the air pressing down on you is air pressure.

Air pressure is not the same everywhere. Sometimes air pressure is low. At other times it can be high.

Lows Temperature affects air pressure. When air gets warmer, gas particles get farther apart. The air gets lighter and rises. Rising air presses down with less force, which creates a low. A low is an area of low air pressure.

The weather here is clear, with a cloudless sky. Air pressure here is likely rising.

Highs When air gets cooler, the gas particles get closer together. The air gets heavier and sinks. It presses down with more force, creating a high. A high is an area of high pressure.

Clouds can't form where air is sinking. So when air pressure gets higher you will often see clear skies. On the other hand, when a low forms, clouds tend to form, and you will often have rain.

Wind Wind is the movement of air from areas of high pressure to areas of low pressure. It's like water running down a hill. When the difference in air pressure is great, wind blows faster. When the difference in pressure is small, wind is slower.

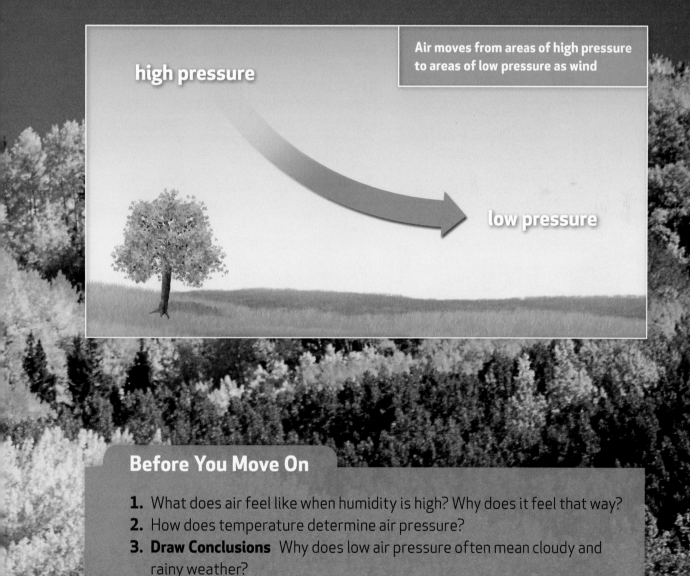

high pressure

Air moves from areas of high pressure to areas of low pressure as wind

low pressure

Before You Move On

1. What does air feel like when humidity is high? Why does it feel that way?
2. How does temperature determine air pressure?
3. **Draw Conclusions** Why does low air pressure often mean cloudy and rainy weather?

The Water Cycle

Water covers more than 70 percent of Earth's surface. Most of Earth's water is in the salt water ocean that covers most of the planet. The ocean is the largest body of water on Earth's surface. Some of Earth's water is also the fresh water in rivers and lakes. Fresh water contains little or no salt. The water in rivers usually flows across Earth's surface. The water in lakes usually does not flow. Some fresh water is frozen as glaciers and ice caps. Groundwater is fresh water below Earth's surface.

Humans use a lot of water. But Earth's supply never runs out because the **water cycle** is at work. The water cycle is the constant movement of water from Earth's surface to the atmosphere and back again. Through the water cycle all of Earth's bodies of water are connected to one another. Salt water can become fresh water, and fresh water can become salt water. Because of the water cycle, Earth's limited water supply has lasted for billions of years.

The Montauk Point Lighthouse in Long Island, New York, overlooks the Atlantic Ocean. Water evaporates from the Atlantic Ocean and enters into the atmosphere.

evaporation

Evaporation When the sun shines on the ocean, it heats the water. The warmer temperature makes the liquid water change to water vapor, a gas. This change from a liquid to a gas is called **evaporation** .

What happens when water evaporates? Particles of liquid move from the surface of the water to the air above. Water particles are always crashing into each other. When the water gets warmer, the particles gain energy. They crash more often. More water particles escape from the water's surface and enter into the air.

The warmer water is, the faster it evaporates. Evaporation is how water enters Earth's atmosphere. Earth's ocean is the largest source of water for evaporation.

During evaporation, liquid water changes to a gas called water vapor.

evaporation

Icecaps and Glaciers 2%

Groundwater, lakes, rivers and others 1%

Oceans 97%

Most of Earth's water is the salt water of oceans. Less than 3 percent is in glaciers and groundwater. Only a tiny percent of Earth's water is in fresh water surface bodies such as lakes and rivers.

Condensation Early in the morning, you may see tiny drops of water on leaves or blades of grass. This is dew, which is caused when water vapor in the air changes into water droplets. Fog and clouds form from water vapor, too.

When water vapor in the air cools, it condenses. Condensation is the change from a gas to a liquid. In the lower atmosphere, air gets cooler the higher it goes. As air rises, the water vapor condenses into clouds.

When air pressure lowers and warm air rises, clouds often form and rain falls. How does this happen? Warm, humid air near the ground rises. When the water vapor in the air reaches cooler air above, the water vapor can condense.

Clouds do not always produce rain. The shape of clouds can give you a clue. Towering cumulonimbus clouds can bring thunder storms. While smaller puffy cumulus clouds do not usually bring rain.

Compare these cumulus clouds that won't bring rain to the cumulonimbus clouds in the big photo that will.

condensation

Just as water vapor condenses on a surface to form dew, a surface is also needed to form clouds. There are millions of tiny bits of dust in the air. Each tiny speck provides a surface on which water vapor can condense. When water vapor condenses around these specks cloud droplets form.

Cloud droplets are tiny. They are much smaller than rain drops. In fact, it would take one million tiny cloud droplets to make just one drop of rain. The cloud droplets are also very light. So they float on the air in the atmosphere.

The change from water vapor to liquid water is called condensation.

condensation

evaporation

Precipitation Rain, snow, sleet, freezing rain, and hail are types of precipitation that fall from clouds. The type of precipitation depends on the temperature of clouds and the temperature of the air between the clouds and the ground.

Rain Rain often starts in clouds as snow. If the snow falls though air that is above freezing on its way to the ground, it melts. It then hits the ground as drops of rain.

Snow Snow starts in clouds as snow. Unlike rain, snow falls through a layer of air that is below freezing. So it remains snow.

Sleet Sleet starts as snow, too. The snow melts into rain as it falls through a layer of warmer air below the clouds. If there is a layer of freezing air between the warm air and the ground, the rain freezes. It then falls as tiny balls of ice called sleet.

precipitation

When many droplets or crystals of water come together in the clouds, they become heavy. Then they fall to Earth as precipitation.

Freezing Rain Freezing rain forms in almost the same conditions as sleet. But the layer of freezing air near the ground is thinner. When the rain falls through it, there isn't enough time for the water to freeze. Instead, it becomes supercooled. Supercooled water is liquid even though its temperature is below freezing. When this super cold water hits a tree branch or the ground, it turns into a layer of ice.

Hailstones Hailstones are round lumps of ice. They start as small ice pieces in storm clouds. Winds in the clouds bounce them up and down through cloud droplets. The cloud droplets freeze onto the ice, making the hailstones bigger and bigger. When the hailstones are heavy enough, they fall from the cloud.

Water that falls to Earth's surface is called precipitation.

precipitation

condensation

evaporation

The water cycle is completed as water returns to Earth's surface as precipitation. Some falls back into oceans, rivers, and lakes.

Other precipitation that falls on land might become runoff. Runoff is water that does not sink into the soil. It flows over the surface of soil, streets, and sidewalks before returning into streams, lakes, or the ocean.

Water can also seep into soil as well. It then trickles down and becomes part of Earth's supply of underground water. Groundwater flows slowly. Still, it eventually returns to rivers and lakes through underground pathways. It can then evaporate and make its trip through the water cycle again.

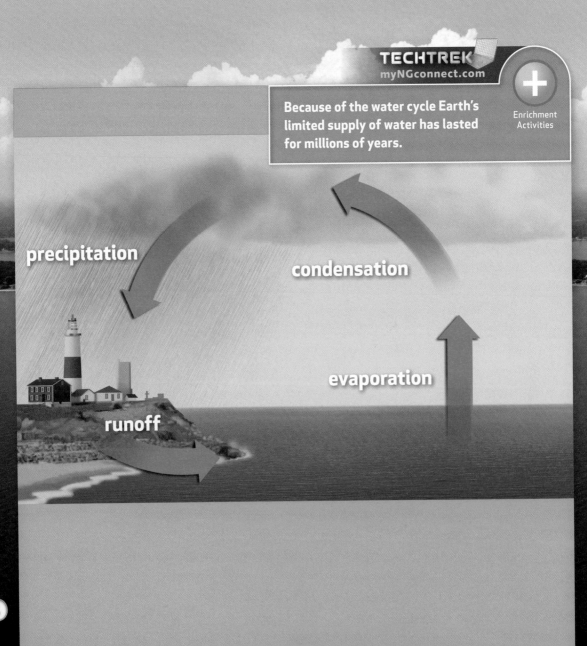

Because of the water cycle Earth's limited supply of water has lasted for millions of years.

precipitation

condensation

evaporation

runoff

Put a layer of gravel or small rocks at the bottom of a clear, plastic container. Cover the gravel with a three-inch layer of sand.

Poke small holes into the bottom of a paper cup with a paper clip. Sprinkle water gently over the sand. This models rain falling on soil. Observe what happens to the water.

How does this show what happens to rain that seeps into the ground?

Before You Move On

1. What is the water cycle?
2. Contrast evaporation and condensation.
3. **Evaluate** Why is the water cycle important for Earth?

Observing Weather Patterns

Scientists observe and study weather patterns to predict the weather in the future. To predict the weather, they use different weather instruments to collect data about the current weather. The chart below shows some of these instruments.

Each instrument in the chart measures just one specific part of the weather, such as temperature. Scientists make their predictions by combining data from many different instruments.

THERMOMETER

Thermometers measure the temperature in degrees. This helps decide how the air will feel and predict weather that could be unsafe.

ANEMOMETER

Anemometers measure wind speed in kilometers or miles per hour. Knowing how fast the wind is blowing can help figure out how much damage a storm may cause.

WIND VANE

Wind vanes measure the direction the wind is blowing: north, east, south, or west. A change in wind direction can mean a change in weather.

HYGROMETER

Hygrometers measure the humidity in the air. Hygrometer readings can show when precipitation may happen, or how uncomfortable the air will feel.

BAROMETER

Barometers measure air pressure. It is also called barometric pressure. Increasing air pressure can mean fair weather. Decreasing air pressure can mean rainy weather.

RAIN GAUGE

Rain gauges measure rainfall in centimeters or inches. Scientists can use rainfall measurements to help predict droughts or floods.

Scientists use other tools, too. Weather satellites show the movement of storms. Weather balloons rise into the sky all over the world each day. They collect data on temperature, air pressure, and humidity. Scientists also use several types of radar to "see" inside clouds. Using radar can help them predict the strength of storms. They can also find clouds that might produce dangerous storms such as tornadoes.

Weather data from thousands of sources goes into computers. The computers hold models that help scientists make forecasts, or predictions. Scientists also make weather maps. The maps show where storms are moving, as well as areas of high and low air pressure.

This meteorologist is using a weather map to help explain his weather forecast.

Air Masses Bring Weather

What's the weather outside? Chances are it's generally the same in a large area surrounding your home. Air moves over Earth's surface as huge masses. In fact, most air masses are more than 1,600 kilometers (1,000 miles) across and several kilometers thick. The temperature and humidity of the air is about the same throughout an air mass. This usually means that the weather, in an air mass, is the same.

But a neighboring air mass may have a different temperature and humidity, and different weather. Knowing what kind of air mass is on the way can help you predict what kind of weather will occur in the near future.

Every air mass takes on the properties of the area where it formed. Some form in cold regions near the poles. These are cold air masses. Others form in warm areas closer to the Equator. Some air masses form over land and others form over water.

Scientists all over the world launch weather balloons twice each day. The balloons carry instruments that gather data at various heights in the atmosphere.

When air masses move they affect the weather of places they pass over. Look at the map. It shows that at any given time, several air masses affect the weather in the United States.

When air masses form over Canada, they are cold and dry. These air masses pass over the northern and central part of the U.S. These parts of the country have cold, dry weather in winter.

Air masses that form over cold polar water bring cold and wet weather to northern coasts. Air masses that form over warm ocean water near the equator bring warm and humid air.

When air masses form over Mexico, they are warm and dry. This is why the Southwest has hot, dry weather.

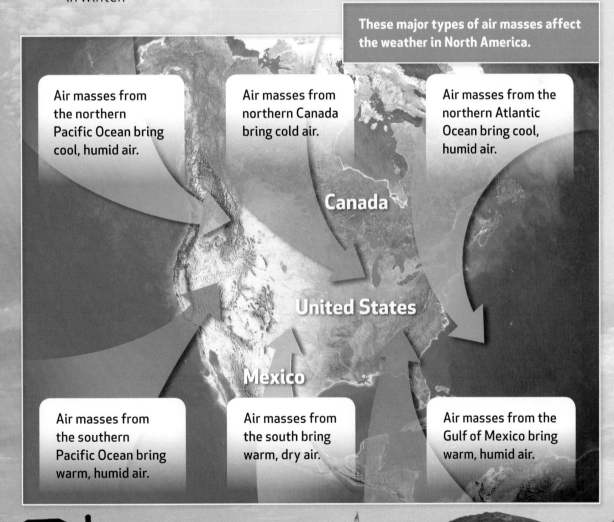

These major types of air masses affect the weather in North America.

Air masses from the northern Pacific Ocean bring cool, humid air.

Air masses from northern Canada bring cold air.

Air masses from the northern Atlantic Ocean bring cool, humid air.

Canada

United States

Mexico

Air masses from the southern Pacific Ocean bring warm, humid air.

Air masses from the south bring warm, dry air.

Air masses from the Gulf of Mexico bring warm, humid air.

Fronts Remember that an air mass has the same temperature and humidity throughout. Some air masses are made up of warm, moist air and some contain cooler, drier air. What happens when two air masses meet? The weather changes. Thunderstorms, rain showers, strong winds and other weather events happen at the boundary between air masses.

The leading edge of an air mass is called a front. The edge of a moving mass of cooler air is a cold front. The edge of a moving mass of warmer air is a warm front

Warm Fronts Warm fronts bring warmer temperatures. At warm fronts, a faster-moving warm air mass meets a cold air mass. The faster, lighter warm air rides up over the heavier cold air. As the warm air rises and cools, the water vapor in the air condenses to form clouds.

At a warm front, the warmer air rises at a low angle. It is like walking up a gradual hill instead of climbing a steep wall. The warm air covers a larger area. The sky fills with thicker, lower clouds and there can be light rain that lasts for hours or days.

TECHTREK
myNGconnect.com

Digital Library

This satellite image shows a front moving over the north Atlantic Ocean.

front

Cold Fronts Cold fronts bring cooler temperatures. Cold fronts form where a faster-moving cold air mass meets a warm air mass. The faster, heavier cold air plows under the warm air. It pushes the warm air up sharply. Water vapor in the rising air condenses to form clouds.

At a cold front, the warmer air rises steeply. It is more like climbing a steep wall than walking up a gradual hill. The rising air cools faster.

It has less area to spread out. Tall storm clouds, called cumulonimbus clouds, may form. These bring short but heavy showers. Sometimes cold fronts bring severe weather, including tornadoes.

Air masses and fronts bring certain types of weather. Scientists can predict this weather by knowing where air masses formed and the track they will take.

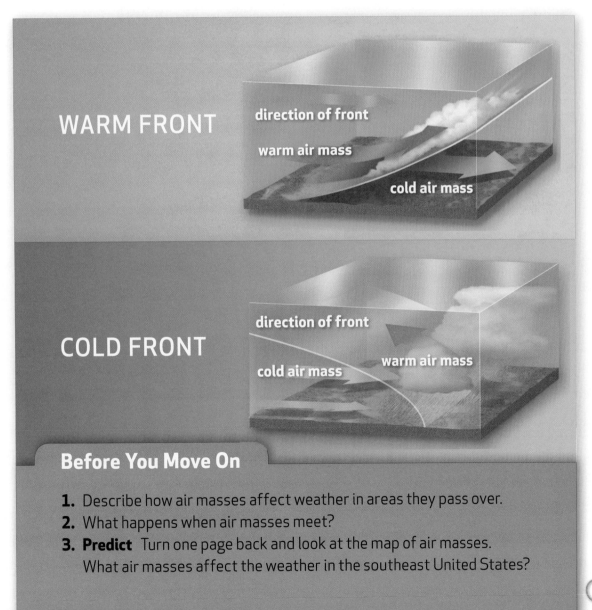

WARM FRONT

direction of front

warm air mass

cold air mass

COLD FRONT

direction of front

cold air mass

warm air mass

Before You Move On

1. Describe how air masses affect weather in areas they pass over.
2. What happens when air masses meet?
3. **Predict** Turn one page back and look at the map of air masses. What air masses affect the weather in the southeast United States?

Climate

When someone says "It is hot and humid here in the summer," they are talking about the **climate** of a particular place. Climate is the general weather of an area over a long period of time. Some places have warmer climates than others. Florida has long, hot summers and warm winters. Alaska has short, cool summers and cold winters.

The climate in Florida is different from the climate in Alaska.

Look at the map of the climate zones of the United States. The range of temperatures and the amount of precipitation a place experiences determines its climate. Each type of climate has certain weather patterns that are the same or repeated year after year.

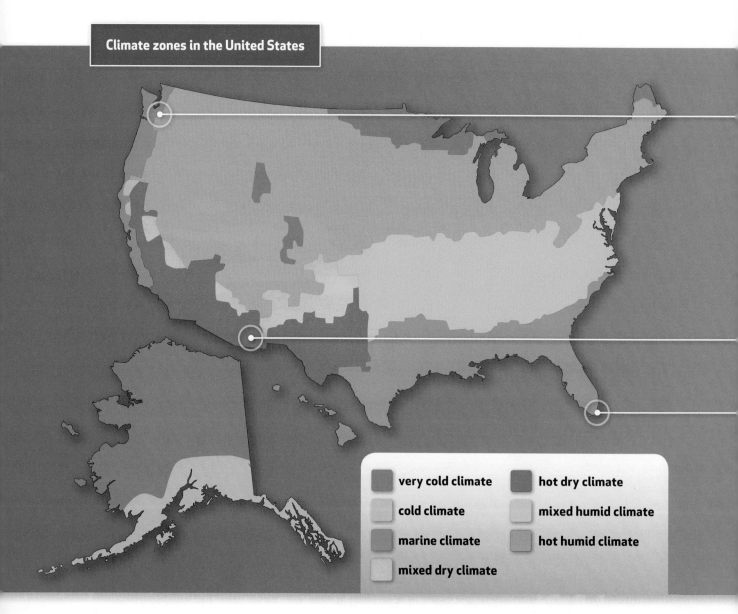

Climate zones in the United States

- very cold climate
- cold climate
- marine climate
- mixed dry climate
- hot dry climate
- mixed humid climate
- hot humid climate

The climate of a region also affects the environment found there. Deserts are usually very dry, but they can be either cold or hot. Swamps usually occur in warm and wet environments.

Mountains can have different climates. The top of a mountain usually has cool temperatures and low humidity. But the base of the mountain has the climate of the surrounding area.

The mountains in Washington State are in a marine climate at the base of the mountains. The temperature goes down as you climb higher.

Picacho Peak State Park near Tuscon, Arizona has a hot, dry climate. The weather in this hot desert is very dry. Less than 25 centimeters (about 10 inches) of rain fall each year.

Southeastern Florida has a hot and humid climate. The swamps of the Everglades contribute to the warm and humid conditions.

Factors Affecting Climate

Average temperature and precipitation are the key parts of every climate. What determines a climate's temperature and precipitation? Latitude, elevation, and nearness to large bodies of water are all factors that can affect climate.

Latitude   Latitude is the distance north or south of the Equator. Latitude affects temperature. Generally it is warmest near the Equator and coolest near the poles. So the closer an area is to the Equator, the warmer its climate.

Elevation   Elevation affects climate, too. Look at the photo. The meadow is green. Why do you think the top of the nearby mountain is covered in snow?

Recall that air gets cooler as it rises. Places that are elevated have cooler temperatures than nearby lowlands. This mountain rises several kilometers above the surrounding land. The temperature on the mountain is much cooler.

Ice and snow cover the top of Mt. Rainier even in summer.

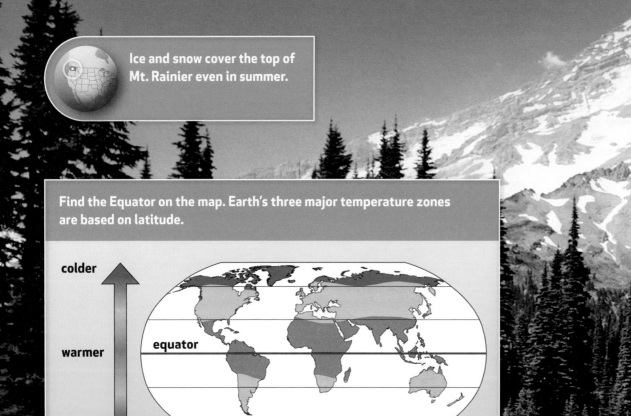

Find the Equator on the map. Earth's three major temperature zones are based on latitude.

colder

warmer

colder

equator

Large Bodies of Water

Temperatures are usually milder near large bodies of water such as oceans and large lakes. Water heats and cools at a slower rate than land. Also, the water does not get as hot or as cold as the land does. How does this affect climate? For example, ocean water heats up during the summer. During the fall the ocean water slowly releases this heat and warms the air. This means that temperatures near the coast may not be as cold as temperatures inland away from the water.

FACTORS THAT AFFECT TEMPERATURE AND PRECIPITATION

FACTOR	ITS EFFECT
LATITUDE	Areas nearest the equator are warmest. Temperature generally decreases toward the poles.
ELEVATION	Climate cools with increasing elevation.
NEARNESS TO LARGE BODIES OF WATER	Large bodies of water moderate the climate of nearby land. Marine climates are milder and have a smaller range of temperature than continental climates.

Comparing Climates Here you can observe two cities with different climates. They are Fargo, North Dakota, and Key West, Florida.

First observe the photo and the data on Fargo. The city is in the northern plains. It is farther from the Equator than Key West. There are no mountains or large bodies of water nearby.

What can you infer about Fargo's climate? Look at the chart on this page. You can see that the hottest month is July and the coldest month is January.

You can see that Fargo's climate is cold and dry in the winter and warmer and more humid in the summer.

Climate Data for Fargo, North Dakota (2008)				
MONTH	AVERAGE HIGH TEMPERATURE		AVERAGE PRECIPITATION	
	°C	(°F)	cm	(in)
JANUARY	−8.9	(15.9)	2.0	(0.8)
FEBRUARY	−5.1	(22.8)	1.5	(0.6)
MARCH	1.8	(35.3)	3.1	(1.2)
APRIL	12.5	(54.5)	3.6	(1.4)
MAY	20.8	(69.5)	6.6	(2.6)
JUNE	25.2	(77.4)	8.9	(3.5)
JULY	27.9	(82.2)	7.4	(2.9)
AUGUST	27.2	(81.0)	6.4	(2.5)
SEPTEMBER	21.1	(69.9)	5.6	(2.2)
OCTOBER	13.4	(56.1)	5.1	(2.0)
NOVEMBER	1.8	(35.2)	2.8	(1.1)
DECEMBER	−6.2	(20.8)	1.5	(0.6)

Fargo is in the very cold climate zone.

Now observe the data for Key West. Key West is an island at the tip of Florida. Key West is closer to the Equator than Fargo. Warm and humid air masses move over it throughout the year. This, along with the warm ocean waters give Key West a warm and humid climate.

You can also see that Key West is wetter than Fargo. Summers are hot and very humid, with frequent afternoon thunderstorms.

Climate Data for Key West, Florida (2008)

MONTH	AVERAGE HIGH TEMPERATURE		AVERAGE PRECIPITATION	
	°C	(°F)	cm	(in)
JANUARY	24.1	(75.3)	5.6	(2.2)
FEBRUARY	24.4	(75.9)	3.8	(1.5)
MARCH	26.0	(78.8)	4.8	(1.9)
APRIL	27.7	(81.9)	5.3	(2.1)
MAY	29.7	(85.4)	8.9	(3.5)
JUNE	31.2	(88.1)	11.7	(4.6)
JULY	31.9	(89.4)	8.4	(3.3)
AUGUST	31.9	(89.4)	13.7	(5.4)
SEPTEMBER	31.2	(88.2)	14.0	(5.5)
OCTOBER	29.3	(84.7)	10.9	(4.3)
NOVEMBER	27.0	(80.6)	6.6	(2.6)
DECEMBER	24.8	(76.7)	5.3	(2.1)

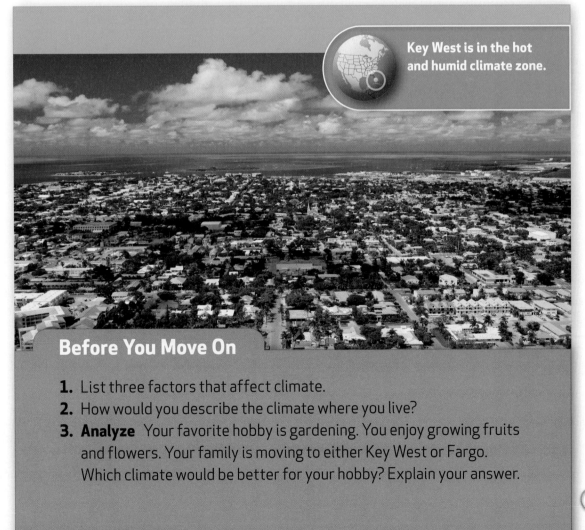

Key West is in the hot and humid climate zone.

Before You Move On

1. List three factors that affect climate.
2. How would you describe the climate where you live?
3. **Analyze** Your favorite hobby is gardening. You enjoy growing fruits and flowers. Your family is moving to either Key West or Fargo. Which climate would be better for your hobby? Explain your answer.

NATIONAL GEOGRAPHIC

THE MONSOON

Each summer, the farmers of India wait for the monsoon. It brings rains they need for their crops. A monsoon is a seasonal change in the direction of the normal wind pattern. The term comes from the Arabic word *mausim*, meaning "season". Monsoons cause wet and dry seasons throughout much of the tropical region.

The winter monsoon brings the dry season. At this time of the year the winds blow to the south. Cool air over India and other parts of Asia pushes south toward the ocean. Because the air comes from over the land, it doesn't have much moisture. Therefore, it doesn't rain much.

In India, the winter monsoon brings clear skies and dry weather.

During the summer monsoon the wind pattern changes direction. Hot temperatures over the land heat the air. Cooler, humid air is blown in from the ocean toward the land. As the cooler, humid air moves inland, it is heated by the warm air. This causes the air to rise, drop its moisture as rain, and be replaced by more cooler humid air moving in from the ocean. This weather pattern repeats until the winds change direction in the fall.

The summer monsoon, which normally produces heavy rains in India, carries moist ocean air over large parts of Asia. During the Northern Hemisphere winter, monsoons bring needed rainfall to Australia and Indonesia. Half the world's population depends on yearly monsoon rains to provide water for crops.

This farmer is preparing a paddy field for rice in the heavy rain of the summer monsoon.

Here is the same location during the summer monsoon. Precipitation has changed the landscape.

Weather occurs in the atmosphere. Many factors affect the weather, including temperature, humidity, and air pressure. The water cycle is responsible for the formation of clouds and precipitation. Scientists use instruments to collect data about all of these factors. They observe weather patterns to predict what the weather will do in the future. Weather patterns over a longer period of time are climate. Climate is affected by different factors, such as latitude, elevation, or nearness to a large body of water.

Big Idea Important weather events are tied to the water cycle.

WEATHER PATTERNS AND EVENTS

THE WATER CYCLE
• evaporation
• condensation
• precipitation

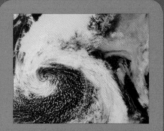

WEATHER
• temperature
• humidity
• wind
• air pressure

CLIMATE
• latitude
• elevation
• nearness to large bodies of water

Vocabulary Review

Match the following terms with the correct definition.

A. weather
B. climate
C. humidity
D. evaporation
E. front
F. water cycle

1. The boundary where two air masses meet
2. The amount of water vapor in the air
3. The change in state from liquid to a gas
4. The pattern of weather over a long period of time
5. The state of the atmosphere at a certain place and time
6. The constant movement of Earth's water from the ground to the atmosphere and back again

Big Idea Review

1. **Name** Name the steps in the water cycle.

2. **Recall** What makes up the atmosphere?

3. **Explain** Why do clear skies often occur over areas of high pressure?

4. **Classify** Which of these does not belong? *hail, runoff, sleet, rain, snow.* Explain your answer.

5. **Make Judgments** The weather forecast states that an area of high pressure is moving into your area. Should you take your umbrella today or leave it at home? Explain your answer.

6. **Analyze** It's a summer day in a city with a desert climate. It's also a summer day in a city near the ocean with a warm, humid climate. How would the day be different in both places, based on the climate?

Write About Weather

Interpreting Diagrams This diagram shows a warm front. Explain what is happening. Then describe the kinds of weather you can expect from a warm front.

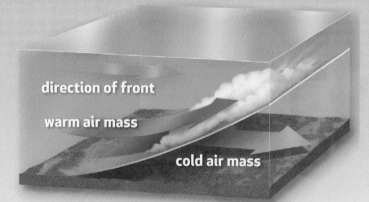

direction of front

warm air mass

cold air mass

CHAPTER 5 — EARTH SCIENCE EXPERT: METEOROLOGIST

What's it like to look inside a storm? Ask a meteorologist.

For people like Sepi Yalda, the sky is a puzzle. How does it change—and how can we predict those changes? Yalda teaches meteorology, the study of weather and the atmosphere.

How did Yalda get interested in the atmosphere? She liked to solve puzzles. "I enjoyed experiments where I wasn't sure of the outcome," she says of what she liked most about science in school. She likes the fact that there are a lot of questions that still need answers in meteorology.

Every day meteorologists answer one big question for all of us. What will the weather be like? To get the answer, they collect data on temperature, winds, humidity, and air pressure. The data comes from hundreds of weather stations. It comes from weather balloons planes, and satellites. Meteorologists put the data into computers that help them make predictions.

People depend on the weather predictions made by meteorologists everyday.

TECHTREK
myNGconnect.com

Student
eEdition

Digital
Library

Yalda is working to find better tools for gathering data and teaching meteorology. "It is always neat to be the first to test a new 3-D tool," she says of a new gadget that lets you visualize flying through winds high up in the atmosphere.

Still, meteorologists do more than predict the weather. They experiment with ways to decrease air pollution. They also provide data that help engineers design buildings and roads, help farmers plan crops, and warn people about storms, floods, and hurricanes.

Think you want to be a meteorologist? Like Yalda, you must earn a degree in meteorology. You will take courses in math, computer science, physics, and chemistry. Many meteorologists work for the government, universities, or radio and TV stations.

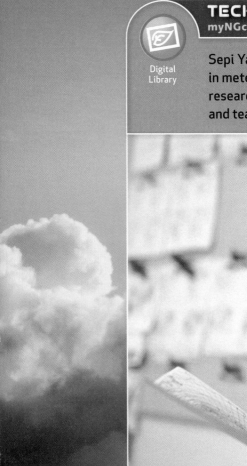

Digital
Library

TECHTREK
myNGconnect.com

Sepi Yalda has a doctorate in meteorology. She does research in meteorology and teaches at a university.

BECOME AN EXPERT

Preparing for Severe Weather

On most days, the information from weather forecasters helps people decide what clothes to wear outdoors, or what outdoor activities to plan. But sometimes weather forecasters perform a much more important task. When weather becomes extreme, they must warn about severe and possibly dangerous weather conditions so that people can prepare and be safe.

Forecasters study data from satellites, radar, and other instruments to try to predict severe weather events. But predictions of extreme weather are not always correct. Weather can change quickly, and in unexpected ways. Ordinary weather patterns can develop into severe storms in days, hours, or even minutes. People living in a storm's path may not have time to leave the area.

Because severe weather can strike quickly, it's important to plan and prepare for it ahead of time. Planning includes knowing what to do and where to go if extreme weather hits. It's also a good idea to have an emergency kit set aside in case you are caught in a storm's path. This kit should have supplies and tools to help you stay safe.

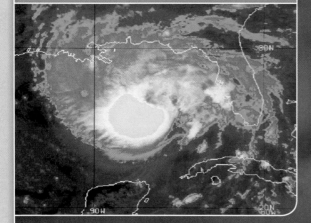

Radar images help forecasters predict severe storms.

TECHTREK
myNGconnect.com

Student
eEdition

Digital
Library

Most weather is not severe enough to cause harm. Yet, high winds flatten houses, floods wash out bridges, and blizzards cover buildings with snow. Severe weather doesn't happen every day. But when it does, people should be ready.

Set aside water, food, and other supplies in case of severe weather.

EMERGENCY SUPPLY KIT

Keep an emergency supply kit handy.

Include:

- Bottled water (enough for 3 days)
- Flashlight
- Battery-powered radio
- Extra batteries for radio and flashlight
- Cell phone with charger
- First aid kit
- Food that won't spoil, such as canned or dry food (enough for 3 days)
- Can opener
- Paper cups, plates, and plastic utensils
- Blankets or sleeping bags (one for each person)
- Matches in waterproof container
- Fire extinguisher
- Pet food (if you have a pet)
- Personal identification
- Credit card and cash
- Extra set of car keys
- Wrench or pliers to turn off utilities
- Whistle or signal flare to signal for help
- Map of your area
- Medications needed by family members
- Any other special items needed by infants, elderly, or disabled persons

Hurricanes In August 2004, Hurricane Charley slammed into Florida. Charley was a destructive storm. Its 233 kilometer (145 mile) per hour winds wrecked thousands of homes and ripped up trees. The storm surge, the dome of water a hurricane pushes in front of it, flooded low areas on the coast.

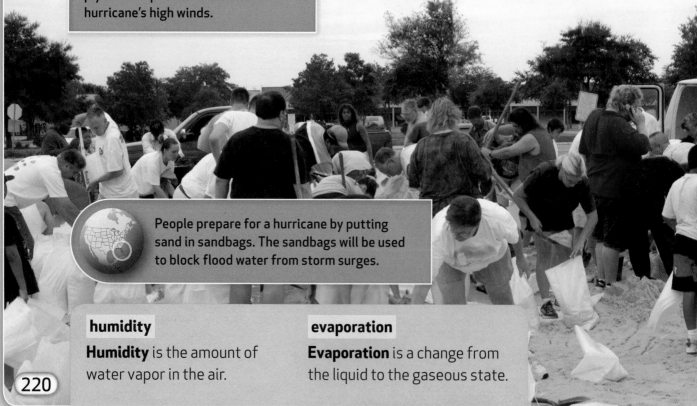

People cover glass windows with plywood to protect them from a hurricane's high winds.

Hurricanes are Earth's biggest storms. They are hundreds of kilometers wide, with winds that can top 250 kilometers (155 miles) per hour. Those that reach the United States form off the west coast of Africa. They develop spiral winds around a center of low pressure. Warm ocean waters and high **humidity** feed the storms. The **evaporation** of humid air from the ocean gives them energy.

When forecasters issue a Hurricane Watch, the storm is still one or two days away. There is a good chance it will hit the area. But it's not a sure thing. To protect their homes, people cover their windows with plywood.

People prepare for a hurricane by putting sand in sandbags. The sandbags will be used to block flood water from storm surges.

humidity
Humidity is the amount of water vapor in the air.

evaporation
Evaporation is a change from the liquid to the gaseous state.

They move items inside that can blow around. They check emergency kits for supplies they will need if power goes out and floodwaters block roads.

A Hurricane Warning means a hurricane will strike. Every family should have an emergency plan. It tells everyone where to go, who to call, and what to do if a storm hits.

As the storm gets closer, those who are in charge will tell people to evacuate. Many of these people live in low areas that flood. Some families go to shelters that keep people safe during the storm. Others choose to remain at home. They stay in interior rooms away from windows and doors.

FAMILY EMERGENCY PLAN INFORMATION

Have a plan to use in case of an emergency, such as a hurricane. Review the plan with your family. List the following information and keep it where you can find it.

• A place where everyone meets in an emergency
• Names and phone numbers of people to contact
• Addresses and phone numbers of family members' work locations and schools
• Name and phone number of family doctor or hospital
• Name and date of birth of each family member
• Any special needs of family members, such as medications or allergies

Hurricanes are ranked on a scale of 1 to 5, with Category 5 storms being the most powerful. This satellite photo shows Charley, a Category 4 storm.

Tornadoes Tornadoes aren't the biggest storms on Earth. Still, they are among the most destructive. Scientists estimate maximum tornado winds at about 402 kilometers (250 miles) per hour. That's strong enough to pull up trees and fling cars around like toys.

Tornadoes often form at **fronts**, as very cold and very warm air masses meet. Powerful thunderstorms form. These storms can form tornadoes.

The conditions for tornado formation are perfect in the middle of the U.S., especially in spring. This area is nicknamed "Tornado Alley" because it gets more tornadoes than any other place.

When forecasters see the conditions that are likely to produce a tornado, they send out a Tornado Watch. People stay tuned to radio and television reports for updates. They also watch the sky because tornadoes can form quickly.

The average wind speed of a tornado is 150 km (96 miles) per hour. But the most powerful tornadoes can have wind speeds of more than 402 km (250 miles) per hour! That's as fast as a jet airplane.

front

A **front** is the boundary where two different air masses meet.

When a tornado is spotted, forecasters issue a Tornado Warning. Often horns or sirens will sound the alarm. People take cover right away. Family emergency plans can help people know where to go and what to do.

TECHTREK
myNGconnect.com

Digital Library

This storm cellar protects a family from deadly tornadoes.

Most families have a room in the house for shelter. The lowest floor is the safest part of the house. Some people huddle in basements. Others pick an interior part of the house away from windows or outside walls. If outside, people lie in flat, low areas away from structures.

Can scientists predict tornadoes? Not exactly. But they have tools for spotting the conditions likely to produce them. Doppler radar can detect air movement within clouds that often means the formation of tornadoes. Scientists can then warn people who might be in their path. As a result, the number of deaths from tornadoes has decreased.

SEVERE WEATHER TERMS

- **Watch:** Conditions are right for severe weather to form. Get prepared. Stay alert. Keep tuned to radio or TV for new information.

- **Warning:** Severe weather will strike your area soon. Take shelter. Evacuate if authorities say to do so.

Winter Storms Northern areas usually have cold **climates** in winter. Snow can be a common sight, but a winter storm is the most severe type of snowfall. These storms can bury roads and buildings. They create cold and icy conditions that are dangerous for people.

Winter storms are not just snowy. They bring extreme cold and high winds ,too. The most severe winter storms can last for days and bring cities to a standstill. Four days of snow in 2001 buried the city of Buffalo, in New York State, under two meters (six feet) of snow!

Snowplow trucks such as this one can spread salt and sand over road surfaces.

climate
Climate is the pattern of weather over a long period of time.

224

There are several types of winter **weather** . A blizzard has heavy snow and winds of at least 56 kilometers (35 miles) per hour. Blowing snow makes it hard to see ahead of you in a blizzard. Nor'easters are winter storms that form along the Atlantic. They blow in a northeast direction. In winter, they bring heavy snow, huge waves, and high winds to the coast.

Forecasters issue Winter Storm Watches when winter storms are possible in a day or two. In areas where winter storms are likely, families should keep an emergency supply kit in the house and in the car. Power failures are common. People must prepare for being stranded without heat or electricity.

A Winter Storm Warning means that the storm will begin soon or has started. Authorities tell people to stay inside. If people go out, they must dress warmly—with hats, mittens, and scarves over their mouths. This weather can be very dangerous because of the extreme cold, wind, ice, and blowing snow.

STORM WARNINGS

WINTER STORM MESSAGE	WHAT IT MEANS
WINTER STORM OUTLOOK	Winter storm conditions are possible in 2–5 days. Listen to TV or radio for storm updates.
WINTER STORM ADVISORY	Winter storm conditions may be hazardous but not severe
WINTER STORM WATCH	Severe winter storm conditions are possible in 36–48 hours. It's time to prepare.
WINTER STORM WARNING	Severe winter storm conditions have begun or will begin within 24 hours. Take steps now to protect yourself.

weather

Weather is the condition of the atmosphere at a certain place and time.

Floods Sometimes the **water cycle** produces more precipitation than usual in a region. Most inland floods happen when rain is so heavy that the ground cannot absorb it. Runoff flows over the ground into streams and rivers. As more and more runoff flows into them, their water level rises. A flood occurs when a stream or river overflows its banks onto land that is normally above water.

Floods can be more severe when the ground is already soggy. Scientists monitor rivers during periods of heavy rain. They can tell when a river is likely to flood. If they issue a Flood Watch, flooding might occur soon. People listen to TV and radio for information. They prepare to leave low areas on the coast or near rivers.

If a Flood Warning is issued, flooding will happen soon. Authorities tell some people to evacuate. If a Flash Flood Warning is issued, people must get to higher ground right away—by car or even on foot. A wall of water can rush down a stream quickly in a flash flood.

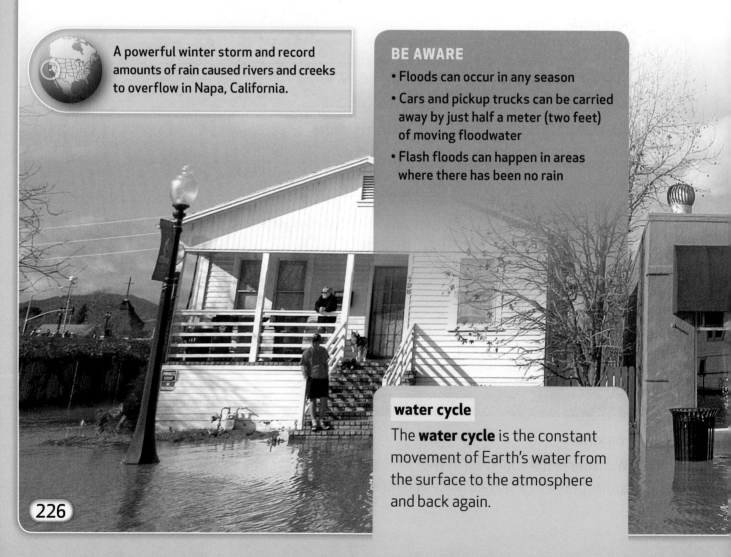

A powerful winter storm and record amounts of rain caused rivers and creeks to overflow in Napa, California.

BE AWARE
- Floods can occur in any season
- Cars and pickup trucks can be carried away by just half a meter (two feet) of moving floodwater
- Flash floods can happen in areas where there has been no rain

water cycle

The **water cycle** is the constant movement of Earth's water from the surface to the atmosphere and back again.

Many people in areas that flood build the first floor of their houses high off the ground. But the best way to prepare for floods is to avoid building in low areas near streams or on beaches. In some places, people no longer put homes, schools, or stores in these places. They are left for parks and land uses that flooding will not damage.

Weather forecasters warn the public about many types of severe weather. As with other severe weather situations, it is best to be prepared. Families should have their own emergency plan. These plans tell everyone what to do in a weather emergency. Families should also have an emergency supply kit.

Scientists use stream-flow gauges to monitor the water level in streams.

People place sandbags along streams to hold back floodwaters.

CHAPTER 5

SHARE AND COMPARE

Turn and Talk Are certain types of severe weather more common in some climates than in others? Form a complete answer to this question together with a partner.

Read Select two pages in this section. Practice reading the pages. Then read them aloud to a partner. Talk about why the pages are interesting.

Write Write a conclusion that tells the important ideas about what you have learned about severe weather. State what you think is the Big Idea of this section. Share what you wrote with a classmate. Compare your conclusions. Did your classmate recall that hurricanes only form over oceans?

Draw Imagine what it would be like to experience a hurricane, flood, blizzard, or tornado. Draw a picture of an activity that you could do to prepare for it. Combine your drawing with those of your classmates to make your own emergency plan.

Glossary

A

apparent motion (uh-PAIR-ant MŌ-shun)
An object's apparent motion is the way it appears to move, not whether or how it actually moves. (p. 12)

atom (AT-uhm)
An atom is the smallest piece of matter than can still be identified as that matter. (p. 98)

B

biomass (BĪ-ō-mas)
Biomass is plant material and animal waste used as fuel. (p. 163)

C

climate (CLĪ-mit)
Climate is the pattern of weather over a long period of time. (p. 206)

crystal (KRIHS-tuhl)
A crystal is a solid that has atoms arranged in a repeating pattern. (p. 98)

D

dwarf planet (DWORF PLA-nit)
A dwarf planet is an object that orbits the sun, is larger than an asteroid and smaller than a planet, and has a nearly round shape. (p. 77)

E

eclipse (i-KLIPS)
An eclipse is the blocking of light shining from one object in space onto another. (p. 30)

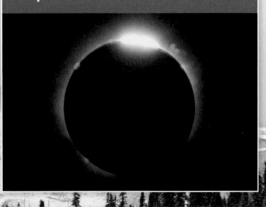

When the moon blocks the sun's light from shining on Earth, a solar eclipse occurs.

The climate of an area determines the plants and animals that live there.

evaporation (ē-va-por-Ā-shun)
Evaporation is a change from the liquid to the gaseous state. (p. 193)

F

fossil fuel (FOS-il FYŪ-ehl)
A fossil fuel is any fuel that formed from the remains of plants and animals that lived millions of years ago. (p. 158)

front (FRUNT)
A front is the boundary where two different air masses meet. (p. 204)

G

galaxy (GA-luk-sē)
A galaxy is a star system that contains large groups of stars. (p. 60)

H

hemisphere (HEM-us-fear)
A hemisphere is one-half of Earth's surface, usually above or below the Equator. (p. 18)

humidity (hyū-MID-it-ē)
Humidity is the amount of water vapor in the air. (p. 189)

Humidity is a main factor that determines weather.

hydroelectric power
(hī-drō-eh-LEK-trik POW-ur)
Hydroelectric power is electricity produced by the energy in moving water. (p. 162)

I

igneous rock (IG-nē-us ROK)
Igneous rock forms when melted rock cools and becomes solid. (p. 106)

Igneous rocks such as granite are often used as building materials for walls and floors.

M

metamorphic rock (met-a-MOR-fik ROK)
Metamorphic rock forms from rock that has been changed by high temperature, high pressure, and hot liquids and gases. (p. 112)

moon (MŪN)
A moon is a large rocky object that orbits a planet. (p. 68)

N

nonrenewable resources
(non-ri-NŪ-ah-bl RĒ-sors-es)
Nonrenewable resources are those that cannot be replaced quickly enough to keep from running out. (p. 139)

O

orbit (OR-bit)
An orbit is the path one object takes around another object. (p. 16)

P

planet (PLA-nit)
A planet is a large nearly round space object that orbits a star. (p. 64)

pollution (puh-LŪ-shun)
Pollution is the presence of substances that are harmful to the environment or living things. (p. 141)

R

renewable resources
(ri-NŪ-ah-bl RĒ-sors-es)
Renewable resources are those that are always being replaced and will not run out. (p. 139)

revolution (rev-u-LŪ-shun)
Revolution is the act of moving around another object. (p. 16)

rock cycle (ROK SĪ-kuhl)
The rock cycle is a series of actions that changes rocks from one type to another. (p. 115)

The melted rock, called lava, will harden into solid rock as part of the rock cycle.

rotation (rō-TĀ-shun)
Rotation is the act of spinning around.
(p. 10)

One complete rotation of Earth
takes 24 hours.

S

sedimentary rock (sed-i-men-tah-rē ROK)
Sedimentary rock forms from small pieces
of rocks and minerals that are cemented
together. (p. 108)

star (STAR)
A star is a ball of hot gases that gives off
light and other types of energy. (p. 58)

U

universe (YŪ-ni-vurs)
The universe is everything that exists
throughout space. (p. 59)

W

water cycle (WAH-tur SĪ-cul)
The water cycle is the constant movement
of Earth's water from the surface to the
atmosphere and back again. (p. 192)

weather (WE-thur)
Weather is the state of the atmosphere
at a certain place and time. (p. 188)

Pieces of rock and minerals were
cemented together to form this
sedimentary rock.

Index

Credits

Front Matter

About The Cover (bg) Whit Richardson/Aurora Photos/Corbis. (t inset) Whit Richardson/Aurora Photos/Corbis. (b inset) David Edwards/National Geographic Image Collection. **ii–iii** Iakov Kalinin/Shutterstock. **iv–v** Jeff Greenberg/Index Stock/age fotostock. **vi–vii** (bg) NASA, NOAO, ESA, the Hubble Helix Nebula Team, M. Meixner (STScI), and T.A. Rector (NRAO). **vii** (t) Carsten Peter/Speleoresearch & Films/National Geographic Image Collection. **viii–ix** (bg) Digital Vision/Getty Images. **ix** (t) David McNew/Getty Images. **x–1** Cotton Coulson/National Geographic Image Collection. **2** (t) Melissa Farlow/National Geographic Image Collection. (c) NASA Goddard Space Flight Center Image by Reto Stöckli (land surface, shallow water, clouds). Enhancements by Robert Simmon (ocean color, compositing, 3D globes, animation). Data and technical support: MODIS Land Group; MODIS Science Data Support Team; MODIS Atmosphere Group; MODIS Ocean Group Additional data: USGS EROS Data Center (topography); USGS Terrestrial Remote Sensing Flagstaff Field Center (Antarctica); Defense Meteorological Satellite Program (city lights). (b) SIME/eStock Photo. **2–3** (bg) NASA, ESA, and The Hubble Heritage Team (STScI/AURA). **3** (t) Sarah Leen/National Geographic Image Collection. (b) Todd Gipstein/National Geographic Image Collection. **4** (t) Jim Webb Photography. (b) Carsten Peter/National Geographic Image Collection.

Chapter 1

5, 6–7 Peter Miller/Stone/Getty Images. **8** (t) Stockbyte/Getty Images. (b) Heiner Heine/imagebroker.net/Photolibrary. **9** Lionel Brown/Image Bank/Getty Images. **10** (l) Barry Rosenthal/The Image Bank/Getty Images. (r) DigitalStock/Corbis. **11** (t) Stockbyte/Getty Images. (b) Sergey Kashkin/iStockphoto. **12–13** Heiner Heine/imagebroker.net/Photolibrary. **14–15** Alan Dyer. **20** (l) Lee Foster/Alamy Images. (r) Steve Baccon/Digital Vision/Getty Images. **21** (t) afplivetwo914126/NewsCom. (b) gary718/Shutterstock. **22** (t) Bill Bachman/Alamy Images. (b) Ian Hamilton/iStockphoto. **23** (l) Jennifer Griner/Shutterstock. (r) Debra James/Shutterstock. **24–25** Alan Novelli/Alamy Images. **26** kristian sekulic/Shutterstock. **28–29** (bg) Chee-Onn Leong/Shutterstock. **30** Lionel Brown/Image Bank/Getty Images. **31** ChinaFotoPress/Getty Images. **32** (bc) Dr. Juerg Alean/Photo Researchers, Inc. (bl), (br) David Woods/Shutterstock. **33** (l, r) Andrew Northrup. **34–35** Melissa Farlow/National Geographic Image Collection. **36–37** (bg) Nancy Camel/Alamy Images. **37** Brian Yarvin/Photo Researchers, Inc. **38** photoHare/Shutterstock. **39** (bg) Steve Cole/Photographer's Choice/Getty Images. (tl) Stockbyte/Getty Images. (tr) Steve and Donna O'Meara/National Geographic Image Collection. **40–41** (bg) kristian sekulic/Shutterstock. **42** (c) NASA Glenn Research Center. **42–43** (bg) NASA Human Space Flight Gallery. **43** (b) NASA Human Space Flight Gallery. **44** Steven Kazlowski/Science Faction/Corbis. **46** Emory Kristof/National Geographic Image Collection. **47** (t) Al Tielemans/Sports Illustrated/Getty Images. (b) WorldFoto/Alamy Images. **48–49** George F. Mobley/National Geographic Image Collection. **50** Jim Keir/Alamy Images. **50–51** (b) George Steinmetz/Corbis. **51** (t) Jeff Harbers/Science Faction/Corbis. **52** WorldFoto/Alamy Images.

Chapter 2

53, 54–55 NASA, ESA, and E. Karkoschka (University of Arizona). **56** (t) T.A. Rector/University of Alaska Anchorage, T. Abbott and NOAO/AURA/NSF. (c) Jim Richardson/National Geographic Image Collection. (b) NASA, ESA, and The Hubble Heritage Team (STScI/AURA). **57** (t) NASA/JPL. (c) Stockbyte/Getty Images. (b) NASA, ESA, H. Weaver (JHU/APL), A. Stern (SwRI), and the

HST Pluto Companion Search Team. **58–59** Jim Richardson/National Geographic Image Collection. **60** NASA, The Hubble Heritage Team and A. Riess (STScI). **60–61** (bg) NASA, ESA, A. Aloisi (STScI/ESA), and The Hubble Heritage (STScI/AURA)-ESA/Hubble Collaboration. **61** NASA, ESA, and The Hubble Heritage Team (STScI/AURA). **62** Jerry Lodriguss/Photo Researchers, Inc. **63** Scott Johnson/Starfire Studios. **66** USGS/Photo Researchers, Inc. **67** NASA/JPL. **68** (t) Stockbyte/Getty Images. (b) NASA Goddard Space Flight Center Image by Reto Stöckli (land surface, shallow water, clouds). Enhancements by Robert Simmon (ocean color, compositing, 3D globes, animation). Data and technical support: MODIS Land Group; MODIS Science Data Support Team; MODIS Atmosphere Group; MODIS Ocean Group Additional data: USGS EROS Data Center (topography); USGS Terrestrial Remote Sensing Flagstaff Field Center (Antarctica); Defense Meteorological Satellite Program (city lights). **69** (bg) Jupiterimages/BrandX/Alamy. (inset) NASA/JPL-Caltech. **70** NASA. **71** (t, b) NASA/JPL/Space Science Institute. **72** Science Source/Photo Researchers, Inc. **73** NASA/JPL. **74–75** NASA/JPL-Caltech/T. Pyle (SSC). **75** NASA/JPL/JHUAPL. **76** (t) NASA, ESA, H. Weaver (JHU/APL), A. Stern (SwRI), and the HST Pluto Companion Search Team. **77** NASA, ESA, J. Parker (Southwest Research Institute), P. Thomas (Cornell University), L. McFadden (University of Maryland, College Park), and M. Mutchler and Z. Levay (STScI)/Space Telescope Science Institute. **78–79** (bg) Ira Meyer/National Geographic Image Collection. **79** Shigemi Numazawa/Atlas Photo Bank/Photo Researchers, Inc. (b) Thomas J. Abercrombie/National Geographic Image Collection. **80** (l) uliyan Velchev/Shutterstock. (c) NASA. (r) Ira Meyer/National Geographic Image Collection. **80–81** (bg) NASA, NOAO, ESA, the Hubble Helix Nebula Team, M. Meixner (STScI), and T.A. Rector (NRAO). **81** NASA/Johns Hopkins University Applied Physics Laboratory/Carnegie Institution of Washington. **82** P. Parviainen/Photo Researchers, Inc. **83** (tl) (c)1997 The Field Museum, GN88132_8c. (tr) Corrin Green. (b) Mark Henle/The Arizona Republic. **84–85** (bg) Kerrick James/Alamy Images. **85** Stephen Alvarez/National Geographic Image Collection. **86** Chris Butler/Photo Researchers, Inc. **87** Shigemi Numazawa/Atlas Photo Bank/Photo Researchers, Inc. **88–89** (b) William K. Hartmann. **89** (t) Randy Olson/National Geographic Image Collection. **90–91** Dan Durda (FIAAA, B612 Foundation). **92** Randy Olson/National Geographic Image Collection.

Chapter 3

93, 94–95 SIME/eStock Photo. **96** (t) Manamana/Shutterstock. (b) Joyce Photographics/Photo Researchers, Inc. **97** (t) Thomas Wiewandt; Visions of America/Corbis. (b) Linda Reinink-Smith/Alamy Images. **98** (bg) Manamana/Shutterstock. (bl) E. R. Degginger/Photo Researchers, Inc. (br) Theodore Gray/Visuals Unlimited. **99** J&L Images/Digital Vision/Getty Images. **100–101** (bg) O.DIGOIT/Alamy Images. **101** (t) Robert Krampf. (b) Wally Eberhart/Visuals Unlimited. **102** (tl) Charles D. Winters/Photo Researchers, Inc. (tr) GC Minerals/Alamy Images. (c) Laitr Keiows/Shutterstock. (bl) GC Minerals/Alamy Images. (br) Sean Curry/iStockphoto. **103** (r1) Biophoto Associates/Photo Researchers, Inc. (r2) Maurice Nimmo; Frank Lane Picture Agency/Corbis. (r3) Joel Arem/Photo Researchers, Inc. (r4) Mark A. Schneider/Photo Researchers, Inc. (r5) Mark Schneider/Getty Images. (r6) Wally Eberhart/Visuals Unlimited. (r7) Only Fabrizio/Shutterstock. (r8) efesan/iStockphoto. (r9) Martin Novak/Shutterstock. **104** (inset) Thomas Wiewandt; Visions of America/Corbis. **104–105** (bg) SEASUN/Shutterstock. **105** (inset) Fenton/Shutterstock. **106** (t) Joyce Photographics/Photo Researchers, Inc. (b) Mark Thiessen/National Geographic Image Collection. **106–107** (bg) imagebroker/Alamy Images. **107** (inset) Glenn Oliver/Visuals Unlimited. **108–109** (bg) James P.

Blair/National Geographic Image Collection. **109** (tl) kudrashka-a/Shutterstock. (tr) Andrew J. Martinez/Photo Researchers, Inc. (cl) John Foxx Images/Imagestate. (cr) Joyce Photographics/Photo Researchers, Inc. (bl) Zirafek/iStockphoto. (br) The Natural History Museum/Alamy Images. **110** (t) Louie Psihoyos/Corbis. (b) Albert J. Copley/Photodisc/Getty Images. **110–111** (bg) Phil Schermeister/National Geographic Image Collection. **112** Linda Reinink-Smith/Alamy Images. **113** (l) Michael P. Gadomski/Photo Researchers, Inc. (r) Marli Miller/Visuals Unlimited. **114–115** imagebroker/Alamy. **115** (t) imagebroker/Alamy. (cl) imagebroker/Alamy Images. (cr) Linda Reinink-Smith/Alamy Images. (bl) John Foxx Images/Imagestate. (br) James P. Blair/National Geographic Image Collection. **116** (bl) Carsten Peter/Speleoresearch & Films/National Geographic Image Collection. **116–117** Carsten Peter/Speleoresearch & Films/National Geographic Image Collection. **117** (b) Ken Lucas/Visuals Unlimited. **118** (l) Zirafek/iStockphoto. (c) O.DIGOIT/Alamy Images. (r) SEASUN/Shutterstock. **118–119** (bg) David McNew/Getty Images. **119** Thomas Wiewandt; Visions of America/Corbis. **120** (t) The Lion's Den Inc. (b) Richard Wilson/Alamy Images. **121** (t, bl, br) The Lion's Den Inc. **122** (l) Phil Schermeister/National Geographic Image Collection. **122–123** (r) Randy Olson/National Geographic Image Collection. **124** (t) Envision/Corbis. (b) NASA Human Space Flight Gallery. **125** (t) Steffen Foerster Photography/Shutterstock. (b) Compassionate Eye Foundation/Tanya Constantine/Getty Images. **126** (t) EugenP/Shutterstock. (b) Ilene MacDonald/Alamy Images. **127** (t) Allison Achauer/iStockphoto. (b) SSPL/Getty Images. **128** (t) Suponev Vladimir Mihajlovich/Shutterstock. **128–129** (b) Ryan McVay/Getty Images. **129** (l) Phil Degginger/Alamy Images. (r) Jeremy Woodhouse/PhotoDisc/Getty Images. **130** (t) Martyn F. Chillmaid/Photo Researchers, Inc. (c) De Agostini Picture Library/Getty Images. (b) Jim Richardson/National Geographic Image Collection. **131** (t) Ashok Rodrigues/iStockphoto. (b) Juan Silva/Iconica/Getty Images. **132** Ilene MacDonald/Alamy Images.

Chapter 4

133, 134–135 Tyrone Turner/National Geographic Image Collection. **136** (t) aceshot1/Shutterstock. (c) James Forte/National Geographic Image Collection. (b) James L. Amos/National Geographic Image Collection. **137** (t) Jim Parkin/Shutterstock. (c) Bill Hatcher/National Geographic Image Collection. (b) Picture Contact/Alamy Images. **138–139** David Kadlubowski/Corbis. **140–141** Brice Dal Farra/Digital Light Source/Peter Arnold, Inc. **142** (c) aceshot1/Shutterstock. **142–143** (bg) James P. Blair/Photodisc/Getty Images. **143** (l) shadowportland/Shutterstock. (r) Jenny E. Ross/Corbis. **144** (l) vrjoyner/Shutterstock. (r) James L. Amos/National Geographic Image Collection. **144–145** (bg) Jim Parkin/Alamy Images. **145** (cl, cr) Andrew Northrup. **146** (c) Corbis Super RF/Alamy Images. **146–147** (bg) Hsing-Wen Hsu/iStockphoto. **147** (t) prettyfoto/Alamy Images. **148–149** Betacam-SP/Shutterstock. **150** (l) Jason Edwards/National Geographic Image Collection. (r) David McNew/Getty Images. **150–151** (bg) JG Photography/Alamy Images. **151** (l) David McNew/Getty Images. (r) Lester Lefkowitz/Getty Images. **152** croftsphoto/Alamy Images. **153** (bg) Jack Sullivan/Alamy Images. (inset) Franz-Peter Tschauner/dpa/Corbis. **154** (t) LWA/Getty Images. (bl) Don Farrall/Getty Images. (br) Stockbyte/Alamy. **155** Leonid Nyshko/Alamy Images. **156–157** Poulides/Thatcher/Stone/Getty Images. **158–159** (bg) James Forte/National Geographic Image Collection. **159** (c) Jim Parkin/Shutterstock. **160** (inset) Sarah Leen/National Geographic Image Collection. **160–161** (bg) Sarah Leen/National Geographic Image Collection. **162** Bill Hatcher/National Geographic Image Collection. **163** Picture Contact/Alamy Images. **164–165** (bg) Corbis Premium RF/Alamy Images. **165** (t) Andrew Penner/iStockphoto. (ct) Sarah Leen/National Geographic Image Collection. (c) Sarah Leen/National Geographic Image Collection. (cb) Bill Hatcher/National Geographic Image Collection. (b) Picture Contact/Alamy Images. **166–167** (l) Tyrone Turner/National Geographic Image Collection.

167 Tyrone Turner/National Geographic Image Collection. **168–169** (bg) Vincenzo Lombardo/Getty Images. **169** Tyrone Turner/National Geographic Image Collection. **170** (b) John Masters/Rebecca Dodder. **170–171** (bg) Dave Reede/AgStock Images/Corbis. **172–173** (bg) Alaska Stock Images/National Geographic Image Collection. **173** (inset) Dennis Finley/National Geographic Image Collection. **174** Paul Burns/Getty Images. **174–175** cycreation/Shutterstock. **176–177** Jeff Greenberg/Index Stock/age fotostock. **177** Directphoto.org/Alamy Images. **178–179** Bill Hatcher/National Geographic Image Collection. **179** Jeff Randall/Getty Images. **180** Jeff Greenberg/Index Stock/age fotostock.

Chapter 5

181, 182–183 Todd Gipstein/National Geographic Image Collection. **184** (t) BrandX/Jupiterimages. (c) Owen Franken/Corbis. (b) Jerry and Marcy Monkman/EcoPhotography.com. **185** (t) Sylvana Rega/Shutterstock. (b) Skip Higgins of Raskal Photography/Alamy Images. **186–187** Digital Vision/Getty Images. **188–189** (bg) Jeremy Woodhouse/Blend Images/Alamy Images. **189** Owen Franken/Corbis. **190–191** BrandX/Jupiterimages. **192–193** Sylvana Rega/Shutterstock. **194** (inset) Duncan Walker/iStockphoto. **194–195** (bg) John Foxx Images/Imagestate. **196–197** Jerry and Marcy Monkman/EcoPhotography.com. **198–199** (bg) Al Braden/Alamy Images. **199** (l, r) Andrew Northrup. **200** (t) Patrick J. Endres/Visuals Unlimited. (tc) parema/iStockphoto. (tb) Jason Cheever/Shutterstock. (bt) saied shahin kiya/Shutterstock. (bc) Palto/Shutterstock. (b) Visuals Unlimited. **201** Image Source/Photolibrary. **202–203** Nick Caloyianis/National Geographic Image Collection. **204** National Remote Sensing Centre Ltd/Photo Researchers, Inc. **207** (t) WorldFoto/Alamy Images. (c) Skip Higgins of Raskal Photography/Alamy Images. (b) Hanne & Jens Eriksen/Minden Pictures. **208–209** PhotoDisc/Getty Images. **210** Patsy Lynch/FEMA. **211** Cameron Davidson/Alamy Images. **212** Lynsey Addario/National Geographic Image Collection. **212–213** (bg) Lynsey Addario/National Geographic Image Collection. **213** Mike Goldwater/Alamy Images. **214** (l) John Foxx Images/Imagestate. (c) National Remote Sensing Centre Ltd/Photo Researchers, Inc. (r) Jeremy Woodhouse/Blend Images/Alamy Images. **214–215** (bg) Jules Frazier/Photodisc/Getty Images. **216** (inset) Sepi Yalda. **216–217** (bg) Iakov Kalinin/Shutterstock. **217** Sepi Yalda. **218** (inset) Ilene MacDonald/Alamy Images. **218–219** (bg) Jim McKinley/Flickr/Getty Images. **219** (inset) Alan Diaz/AP Images. **220** (t) Charles W. Luzier/Reuters/Corbis. **220–221** (bl) PhotoStockFile/Alamy Images. **221** (br) NASA/Goddard Space Flight Center/Scientific Visualization Studio. **222–223** (bg) Digital Vision/Getty Images. **223** Jim Sigmon/Dallas Morning News/NewsCom. **224** (t) Sean Donohue Photo/Shutterstock. (b) China Photos/Getty Images. **226–227** (b) David Paul Morris//Getty Images. **227** (tl) Bradley C Bower/AP Images. (tr) Sun-Star, Jack Bland/AP Images. **228** Digital Vision/Getty Images.

End Matter

EM1 (t) Lionel Brown/Image Bank/Getty Images. (b) PhotoDisc/Getty Images. **EM2** (t) Joyce Photographics/Photo Researchers, Inc. (b) Owen Franken/Corbis. **EM3** imagebroker/Alamy. **EM4** (t) Stockbyte/Getty Images. (b) James P. Blair/National Geographic Image Collection. **EM8** Compassionate Eye Foundation/Tanya Constantine/Getty Images. **EM11** (l) GC Minerals/Alamy Images. (r) Sean Curry/iStockphoto. **EM12–EM13** James P. Blair/Photodisc/Getty Images. **EM16** Jeremy Woodhouse/Blend Images/Alamy Images. **Back Cover** (bg) Whit Richardson/Aurora Photos/Corbis. (tl) Robert Clark/National Geographic Image Collection. (tr) Carsten Peter/National Geographic Image Collection. (c) NOAA/Getty Images. (bl) Gay Bumgarner/Photographer's Choice/Getty Images. (br) Carsten Peter/National Geographic Image Collection.